ROYAL COURT

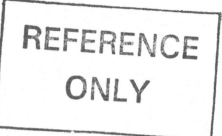

Royal Court Theatre presents

THE FORCE OF CHANGE

by **Gary Mitchell**

First performed at the Royal Court Jerwood Theatre Upstairs,
Sloane Square, London on 6 April 2000

First performance at the Royal Court Jerwood Theatre Downstairs,
Sloane Square, London on 2 November 2000

THE FORCE OF CHANGE

by **Gary Mitchell**

Cast in order of appearance
Bill Byrne **Sean Caffrey**
Caroline Patterson **Laine Megaw**
Mark Simpson **Simon Wolfe**
David Davis **Stuart Graham**
Stanley Brown **Stephen Kennedy**
Rabbit **Gerard Jordan**

Director **Robert Delamere**
Designer **Simon Higlett**
Sound Designer **Paul Arditti**
Lighting Designer **Chris Davey**
Composer **Harry Peat**
Assistant Director **Janice Dunn**
Casting Director **Lisa Makin and Julia Horan**
Production Manager **Paul Handley**
Company Stage Manager **Cath Binks**
Stage Management **Abi Coyle, Charlotte E. Padgham, Tamara Albachari**
Costume Supervisor **Suzanne Duffy**
Dialect Coach **Majella Hurley**
Company Voice Work **Patsy Rodenburg**

Royal Court Theatre would like to thank the following for their help with this production:
Wardrobe care by Persil and Comfort courtesy of Lever Brothers Ltd.

THE COMPANY

Gary Mitchell (writer)
For the Royal Court: Trust.
Other theatre includes: Marching On, Tearing the
Loom (Lyric, Belfast); Energy (Playhouse,
Londonderry); As the Beast Sleeps (National
Theatre Society/Abbey, Dublin); In a Little World of
Our Own (Lyric, Belfast/National Theatre
Society/Abbey, Dublin/Donmar); Sinking, That
Driving Ambition (Replay Theatre Company).
Films under commission: Once Upon a Time in
Belfast (DNA Films).
Television includes: As the Beast Sleeps (in
development); Red, White and Blue (BBC);
An Officer from France (RTE).
Radio includes: Drumcree, Independent Voice,
The World, The Flesh and the Devil, Poison Hearts
(BBC Radio 4); Stranded (BBC Radio 3).
Awards include: Joint winner of the George Devine
Award 2000 for The Force of Change. Pearson
Best Play Award 1999 for Trust, Irish Times
Theatre Award for Best New Play 1997 and Belfast
Arts Drama Award 1998 for In a Little World of
Our Own, Belfast Arts Drama Award 1998 for
Sinking, Stewart Parker Award 1994 for
Independent Voice, BBC Radio 4 Young
Playwrights Festival Award for The World, the
Flesh and the Devil.

Paul Arditti (sound designer)
Paul Arditti has been designing sound for theatre
since 1983. He currently combines his post as
Head of Sound at the Royal Court (where he has
designed more than 60 productions) with regular
freelance projects.
For the Royal Court: My Zinc Bed, 4.48 Psychosis,
Fireface, Mr Kolpert, The Force of Change, Hard
Fruit, Other People, Dublin Carol, Breath, Boom,
The Kitchen, Rat in the Skull, Some Voices, Mojo,
The Lights, The Weir; The Steward of
Christendom, Shopping and Fucking, Blue Heart
(co-production with Out of Joint); The Chairs
(co-production with Theatre de Complicite); The
Strip, Neverland, Cleansed, Via Dolorosa, Real
Classy Affair.
Other theatre includes: Light (Complicite); Our
Lady of Sligo (RNT with Out of Joint); Some
Explicit Polaroids (Out of Joint); Hamlet, The
Tempest (RSC); Orpheus Descending, Cyrano de
Bergerac, St Joan (West End); Marathon (Gate).
Musicals includes: Doctor Dolittle, Piaf, The
Threepenny Opera.
Awards include: Drama Desk Award for
Outstanding Sound Design 1992 for Four Baboons
Adoring the Sun (Broadway).

Sean Caffrey
For the Royal Court: The Force of Change
(April 2000).
Other theatre includes: Marching On,
Spokesong, Over the Bridge, The Gigli
Concert, The Hidden Curriculum, The
Taming of the Shrew, She Stoops to Conquer,
Volunteers, Feast of Lupercal, Lengthening
Shadows (Lyric, Belfast); I Won't Dance, Don't
Ask Me, Joe the Blow from Sandy Row
(Ireland tour); Tom & Jerry (Lyric, Belfast
Festival).
Television includes: Z-Cars, Softly Softly, Paul
Temple, No Hiding Place, Coronation Street,
Harry's Game, Edge of Darkness, Crossfire,
Covington Cross, Force of Duty, The Bill.
Film includes: The Bedford Incident, I Was
Happy Here, When Dinosaurs Ruled the
Earth, The Viking Queen, Run with the Wind,
The Human Factor, Ascendency, The First
Olympics, Resurrection Man, Divorcing Jack.
Sean has his own theatre company in
Belfast - North Face.

Chris Davey (lighting designer)
For the Royal Court: The Force of Change
(April 2000).
Theatre includes: The Car Man, Shining Souls
(Old Vic); God Only Knows (Tour and West
End); Closer (Abbey, Dublin); Baby Doll
(Albery, RNT, Birmingham Rep); Black Goes
with Everything (Churchill, Bromley); Anna
Karenina (Gothenburg); Three Sisters
(Whitehall); The Way of the World, A Woman
of No Importance, Nude with Violin, The
Illusion (Royal Exchange, Manchester); The
Colour of Justice (RNT, Victoria Palace, West
Yorkshire Playhouse); The Deep Blue Sea
(Royal Lyceum, Edinburgh); Passing Places
(Traverse, Edinburgh); Cause Celebre, Then
Again... (Lyric, Hammersmith); Brothers of
the Brush (Everyman, Liverpool); In a Little
World of Our Own (Donmar); Blood
Wedding, Grimm Tales (Young Vic); Just One
World (Aachen, Germany); Sweeney Todd, Of
Thee I Sing (Bridewell); A Midsummer Night's
Dream, Everyman (RSC and New York); The
Comedy of Errors (RSC and world tour);
Romeo and Juliet, A Month in the Country,
Troilus and Cressida, Easter (RSC); War and
Peace (Shared Experience and RNT); Jane
Eyre, Anna Karenina, The Tempest, Desire
Under the Elms, Mill on the Floss, The
Danube (Shared Experience).
Opera includes: The Picture of Dorian Gray
(Opera de Monte Carlo); Gli Equivoci Nel
Sebiante (Batignano Opera, Tuscany).

Robert Delamere (director)
Associate director of ACT Productions.
For the Royal Court: Force of Change (April
2000), Neverland (as producer for The
Foundry).
Other theatre for The Foundry includes: In a
Little World of Our Own (Donmar); The
Knocky, Happy Valley (Everyman, Liverpool).
Other theatre includes: Brothers of the Brush
(Everyman, Liverpool); What the Butler Saw,
Tartuffe, Julius Caeser (Royal Exchange,
Manchester); Jane Eyre, Playboy of the Western
World, The Crucible (Crucible, Sheffield); Les
Liaisons Dangereuses (Teatro Nacional S.Joao,
Portugal); Pinnochio in Venice (National Theatre
of Craiova, Romania).
As artistic director of Ragazzi: The Shoemaker's
Wonderful Wife, The Puppet Play of Don
Cristobel, Buster Keaton's Spin, The Inkwell,
Peter and the Captain, When Five Years Pass
(BAC).
Opera includes: I Giganti Della Montagne, San
Giovanni Battista (Batigano Opera Festival, Italy).
TV includes: Brookside.
Awards include: Edinburgh Festival Fringe First
Award for When Five Years Pass.

Janice Dunn (assistant director)
Theatre includes: Road, Sparkleshark, Guys and
Dolls, Chicago, Jack and the Beanstalk, It's a
Lovely Day Tomorrow (Belgrade Theatre,
Coventry). She will also be directing a Christmas
production for the Mercury Theatre, Colchester.
Janice is the Director of Mad Half-Hour Theatre
Company in Coventry.

Stuart Graham
For the Royal Court: The Force of Change (April
2000).
Other theatre includes: Carthiginians, How
Many Miles to Babylon, The Tempest, Great
Expectations, Noises Off, Dockers, Hamlet,
Rebecca (Lyric, Belfast); In a Little World of Our
Own, As the Beast Sleeps, The Well of Saints,
Observe the Sons of Ulster (Abbey, Dublin); In a
Little World of Our Own (The Foundry,
Donmar Warehouse); Northern Star, New
Morning (Rough Magic); Brothers of the Brush
(Arts); The Silver Tassie (Almeida); Alternative
Future (Belfast/Glasgow); Keely and Du
(Olympia).
Television includes: Shockers II Cyclops, The
Sins, The Governor, Love Lies Bleeding, Active
Defence.
Film includes: The Devil You Know, Misery
Harbour, Fatal Extraction, One Man's Hero,
Racing Homer, The Butcher Boy, The Informant,
Michael Collins, The Bargain Shop.

Simon Higlett (designer)
For the Royal Court: The Force of Change (April
2000)
Other theatre includes: Long Day's Journey into
Night, The Accused, The Chiltern Hundreds, A
Song at Twilight (West End); Beyond a Joke
(tour); The Country Wife (Shakespeare Theatre,
Washington DC); Mrs Warren's Profession, Peer
Gynt (Manchester Royal Exchange); The
Barchester Chronicles, Our Betters, Beethoven's
Tenth, Mansfield Park, The Miser, A Doll's
House, Rope, Dangerous Corner, Three Sisters,
Scenes from a Marriage (Chichester); The
Prisoner of Second Avenue, Antony and
Cleopatra, The Taming of the Shrew, Lady
Windemere's Fan (Haymarket); Talking Heads
(Comedy); Kean (Old Vic); Medea (Young Vic);
Singer (RSC); The Magistrate (The Savoy); In a
Little World of Our Own (Donmar); The Ride
Down Mount Morgan (Derby).
Opera includes: Resurrection (Houston Grand
Opera); The Barber of Seville (Germany); Don
Giovanni, La Traviata, La Cenerentola, The
Marriage of Figaro, The Magic Flute (Music
Theatre London).
Simon was Head of Design at the New
Shakespeare Company from 1986 to 1989.

Gerard Jordan
For the Royal Court: The Force of Change (April
2000).
Other theatre includes: Rock Nativity, Oliver,
Joseph (Corpus Christi).
Television includes: Gun, Active 8, Over the Wall,
Hospice Promotional Video.
Film includes: Boxed, Accelerator, Divorcing
Jack.

Stephen Kennedy

For the Royal Court: The Force of Change (April 2000).

Other theatre includes: Juno and the Paycock (Donmar); Measure for Measure, Shadows - Riders to the Sea, Purgatory, The Shadows of the Glen (RSC); This Lime Tree Bower (RSC Fringe); Macbeth (Kilkenny Castle); Translations (Royal Lyceum, Edinburgh); Phaedra (Gate, Dublin); Double Helix, On the Outside, Silverlands, Gadia Gear na Geamh Oiche, On the Inside, Away Alone (Peacock, Dublin); Miss Julie (Andrew's Lane); The Taming of the Shrew (Lyric, Belfast); Belfry (Druid); Hamlet, The Honey Spike (Abbey, Dublin); Donny Boy (Tinderbox Theatre Company).

Television includes: Shockers II, King of the Bongo, Father Ted, Ballykissangel, The Hanging Gale, The Snapper.

Film includes: Nothing Personal, Braveheart, Sylvester.

Laine Megaw

For the Royal Court: Trust.

Other theatre includes: Aristocrats (Chichester Festival Theatre); The Merchant of Venice (Waterfront Theatre Irish tour); An Ideal Husband (Galloglass Theatre Co. Irish tour); The Merchant of Venice, Over the Bridge, New Morning, Rough Beginnings, Marching On (Lyric, Belfast); Bell, Book & Candle, The House of Goodwill, Holly & The Lollypop Lady (Centre Stage Theatre Co.); Cinderella (Arts Theatre, Belfast).

Film includes: Divorcing Jack, The Devil You Know, Anno Domini, Sunset Height.

Harry Peat (composer)

Orchestral work includes: Orchestrator for composer Jaz Coleman (Orchestral Doors Album); Orchestrator for composer Tolga Kashif for Turkish Relief Fund (Barbican).

Pop includes: Recording under artist name "HP Source" with Red Parrot Recordings; licenses under artist name "Nimbus" to Cafe del Mar 20th Anniversary compilation and Chillout 2000 compilation.

Television includes: Sky News and History Channel idents, Sky Digital campaign (Sky TV); Correspondent titles (BBC); Always and Everyone incidental music (ITV); Tinsel Town (BBC).

Simon Wolfe

Theatre includes: Wonderful Tennessee, Marching On (Lyric, Belfast); The Silver Lake (Wilton's Music Hall); Outside On the Street (Gate); Waiting for Godot (Teatro Nationale, Milan); Therese Raquin (The White Bear); The Changing Room (Duke of York's); The Traitor (Bridewell); Hereward the Wake (Theatre Royal, Norwich); The Corsican Brothers (Abbey, Dublin); At Our Table (RNT); Volpone (Almeida).

Television includes: The Great Kandinsky, The Bill.

THE ENGLISH STAGE COMPANY
AT THE ROYAL COURT

The English Stage Company at the Royal Court
opened in 1956 as a subsidised theatre
producing new British plays, international plays
and some classical revivals.

The first artistic director George Devine aimed
to create a writers' theatre, 'a place where the
dramatist is acknowledged as the fundamental
creative force in the theatre and where the play
is more important than the actors, the director,
the designer'. The urgent need was to find a
contemporary style in which the play, the acting,
direction and design are all combined. He
believed that 'the battle will be a long one to
continue to create the right conditions for
writers to work in'.

Devine aimed to discover 'hard-hitting,
uncompromising writers whose plays are
stimulating, provocative and exciting'. The Royal
Court production of John Osborne's Look Back
in Anger in May 1956 is now seen as the decisive
starting point of modern British drama, and the
policy created a new generation of British
playwrights. The first wave included John
Osborne, Arnold Wesker, John Arden, Ann
Jellicoe, N F Simpson and Edward Bond. Early
seasons included new international plays by
Bertolt Brecht, Eugène Ionesco, Samuel Beckett,
Jean-Paul Sartre and Marguerite Duras.

The theatre started with the 400-seat
proscenium arch Theatre Downstairs, and then
in 1969 opened a second theatre, the 60-seat
studio Theatre Upstairs. Productions in the
Theatre Upstairs have transferred to the West
End, such as Conor McPherson's The Weir,
Kevin Elyot's My Night With Reg and Ariel
Dorfman's Death and the Maiden. The Royal
Court also co-produces plays which have
transferred to the West End or toured
internationally, such as Sebastian Barry's The
Steward of Christendom and Mark Ravenhill's
Shopping and Fucking (with Out of Joint), Martin
McDonagh's The Beauty Queen Of Leenane
(with Druid Theatre Company), Ayub Khan-
Din's East is East (with Tamasha Theatre
Company, and now a feature film).

Since 1994 the Royal Court's artistic policy has
again been vigorously directed to finding and
producing a new generation of playwrights. The
writers include Joe Penhall, Rebecca Prichard,
Michael Wynne, Nick Grosso, Judy Upton,
Meredith Oakes, Sarah Kane, Anthony Neilson,
Judith Johnson, James Stock, Jez Butterworth,
Marina Carr, Simon Block, Martin McDonagh,
Mark Ravenhill, Ayub Khan-Din, Tamantha
Hammerschlag, Jess Walters, Che Walker, Conor
McPherson, Simon Stephens, Richard Bean, Roy

photo: Andy Chopping

Williams, Gary Mitchell, Mick Mahoney, Rebecca
Gilman, Christopher Shinn, Kia Corthron, David
Gieselmann, Marius von Mayenburg and David
Eldridge. This expanded programme of new
plays has been made possible through the
support of A.S.K Theatre Projects, the Jerwood
Charitable Foundation, the American Friends of
the Royal Court and many in association with the
Royal National Theatre Studio.

In recent years there have been record-
breaking productions at the box office, with
capacity houses for Jez Butterworth's Mojo,
Sebastian Barry's The Steward of Christendom,
Martin McDonagh's The Beauty Queen of
Leenane, Ayub Khan-Din's East is East, Eugène
Ionesco's The Chairs, David Hare's My Zinc Bed
and Conor McPherson's The Weir, which
transferred to the West End in October 1998
and ran for nearly two years at the Duke of
York's Theatre.

The newly refurbished theatre in Sloane Square
opened in February 2000, with a policy still
inspired by the first artistic director George
Devine. The Royal Court is an international
theatre for new plays and new playwrights, and
the work shapes contemporary drama in Britain
and overseas.

REBUILDING THE ROYAL COURT

In 1995, the Royal Court was awarded a National Lottery grant through the Arts Council of England, to pay for three quarters of a £26m project to completely rebuild our 100-year old home. The rules of the award required the Royal Court to raise £7.6m in partnership funding. The building has been completed thanks to the generous support of those listed below. We are particularly grateful for the contributions of over 5,700 audience members.

If you would like to support the ongoing work of the Royal Court, please contact the Development Department on 020 7565 5050.

ROYAL COURT
DEVELOPMENT BOARD
Elisabeth Murdoch (Chair)
Jonathan Cameron (Vice Chair)
Timothy Burrill
Anthony Burton
Jonathan Caplan QC
Monica Gerard-Sharp
Joyce Hytner
Dany Khosrovani
Feona McEwan
Michael Potter
Sue Stapely
Charlotte Watcyn Lewis

PRINCIPAL DONOR
Jerwood Foundation

WRITERS CIRCLE
Sky
The Cadogan Estate
Carillon/Schal
News International plc
Pathé
The Eva and Hans K Rausing Trust
The Rayne Foundation
Garfield Weston Foundation

DIRECTORS CIRCLE
The Esmée Fairbairn Charitable Trust
The Granada Group plc

ACTORS CIRCLE
Edward C Cohen & The Blessing Way
Foundation
Ronald Cohen & Sharon Harel-Cohen
Quercus Charitable Trust
The Basil Samuel Charitable Trust
The Trusthouse Charitable Foundation
The Woodward Charitable Trust

SPECIFIC DONATIONS
The Foundation for Sport and the Arts for Stage System
John Lewis Partnership plc for Balcony
City Parochial Foundation for Infra Red Induction Loops and Toilets for Disabled Patrons
RSA Art for Architecture Award Scheme for Antoni Malinowski Wall Painting

STAGE HANDS CIRCLE
Abbey National Charitable Trust
Anonymous
Miss P Abel Smith
The Arthur Andersen Foundation
Associated Newspapers Ltd
The Honorable M L Astor Charitable Trust
Rosalind Bax
Character Masonry Services Ltd
Elizabeth Corob
Toby Costin
Double O Charity
The D'Oyly Carte Charitable Trust
Thomas & Simone Fenton
Lindy Fletcher
Michael Frayn
Susan & Richard Hayden
Mr R Hopkins
Roger Jospé
William Keeling
Lex Service plc
Miss A Lind-Smith
The Mactaggart Third Fund
Fiona McCall
Mrs Nicola McFarland
Mr J Mills
The Monument Trust
Jimmy Mulville & Denise O'Donoghue
David Murby
Michael Orr
William Poeton CBE & Barbara Poeton
Angela Pullen
Mr & Mrs JA Pye's Charitable Settlement
Ruth & Richard Rogers
Ann Scurfield
Ricky Shuttleworth
Brian Smith
The Spotlight
Mr N Trimble
Lionel Wigram Memorial Trust
Madeline Wilks
Richard Wilson
Mrs Katherine Yates

DESIGN TEAM
Haworth Tompkins Architects
Tony Hudson
Theatre Projects Consultants
Schal Construction Management
Price & Myers
Max Fordham & Partners
Paul Gillieron Acoustic Design
Mark Henderson
The Peter Burholt Partnership
Centre for Accessible Environments
Citex Bucknall Austin
Arnold Project Services
Drivers Jonas
Michael Gallie & Partners
Montressor Partnership

PROGRAMME SUPPORTERS

The Royal Court (English Stage Company Ltd) receives its principal funding from the London Arts Board. It is also supported financially by a wide range of private companies and public bodies and earns the remainder of its income from the box office and its own trading activities. The Royal Borough of Kensington & Chelsea gives an annual grant to the Royal Court Young Writers' Programme and the London Boroughs Grants Committee provides project funding for a number of play development initiatives.

Royal Court Registered Charity number 231242.

This year the Jerwood Charitable Foundation continues to support new plays by new playwrights with the fifth series of Jerwood New Playwrights. Since 1993 the A.S.K. Theater Projects of Los Angeles has funded a Playwrights' Programme at the theatre. Bloomberg Mondays, a continuation of the Royal Court's reduced price ticket scheme, is supported by Bloomberg News. BSkyB has also generously committed to a two-year sponsorship of the Royal Court Young Writers' Festival.

AWARDS FOR THE ROYAL COURT

Ariel Dorfman's Death and the Maiden and John Guare's Six Degrees of Separation won the Olivier Award for Best Play in 1992 and 1993 respectively. Terry Johnson's Hysteria won the 1994 Olivier Award for Best Comedy, and also the Writers' Guild Award for Best West End Play. Kevin Elyot's My Night with Reg won the 1994 Writers' Guild Award for Best Fringe Play, the Evening Standard Award for Best Comedy, and the 1994 Olivier Award for Best Comedy. Joe Penhall was joint winner of the 1994 John Whiting Award for Some Voices. Sebastian Barry won the 1995 Writers' Guild Award for Best Fringe Play, the 1995 Critics' Circle Award and the 1997 Christopher Ewart-Biggs Literary Prize for The Steward of Christendom, and the 1995 Lloyds Private Banking Playwright of the Year Award. Jez Butterworth won the 1995 George Devine Award for Most Promising Playwright, the 1995 Writers' Guild New Writer of the Year Award, the Evening Standard Award for Most Promising Playwright and the 1995 Olivier Award for Best Comedy for Mojo. Phyllis Nagy won the 1995 Writers' Guild Award for Best Regional Play for Disappeared.

The Royal Court won the 1995 Prudential Award for Theatre and was the overall winner of the 1995 Prudential Award for the Arts for creativity, excellence, innovation and accessibility. The Royal Court Theatre Upstairs won the 1995 Peter Brook Empty Space Award for innovation and excellence in theatre.

Michael Wynne won the 1996 Meyer-Whitworth Award for The Knocky. Martin McDonagh won the 1996 George Devine Award, the 1996 Writers' Guild Best Fringe Play Award, the 1996 Critics' Circle Award and the 1996 Evening Standard Award for Most Promising Playwright for The Beauty Queen of Leenane. Marina Carr won the 19th Susan Smith Blackburn Prize (1996/7) for Portia Coughlan. Conor McPherson won the 1997 George Devine Award, the 1997 Critics' Circle Award and the 1997 Evening Standard Award for Most Promising Playwright for The Weir. Ayub Khan-Din won the 1997 Writers' Guild Award for Best West End Play, the 1997 Writers' Guild New Writer of the Year Award and the 1996 John Whiting Award for East is East. Anthony Neilson won the 1997 Writers' Guild Award for Best Fringe Play for The Censor.

At the 1998 Tony Awards, Martin McDonagh's The Beauty Queen of Leenane (co-production with Druid Theatre Company) won four awards including Garry Hynes for Best Director and was nominated for a further two. Eugene Ionesco's

The Chairs (co-production with Theatre de Complicite) was nominated for six Tony awards. David Hare won the 1998 Time Out Live Award for Outstanding Achievement and six awards in New York including the Drama League, Drama Desk and New York Critics Circle Award for Via Dolorosa. Sarah Kane won the 1998 Arts Foundation Fellowship in Playwriting. Rebecca Prichard won the 1998 Critics' Circle Award for Most Promising Playwright for Yard Gal.

Conor McPherson won the 1999 Olivier Award for Best New Play for The Weir. The Royal Court won the 1999 ITI Award for Excellence in International Theatre. Sarah Kane's Cleansed was judged Best Foreign Language Play in 1999 by Theater Heute in Germany. Gary Mitchell won the 1999 Pearson Best Play Award for Trust. Rebecca Gilman was joint winner of the 1999 George Devine Award and won the 1999 Evening Standard Award for Most Promising Playwright for The Glory of Living. Roy Williams and Gary Mitchell were joint winners of the George Devine Award 2000 for Most Promising Playwright for Lift Off and The Force of Change respectively.

In 1999, the Royal Court won the European theatre prize New Theatrical Realities, presented at Taormina Arte in Sicily, for its efforts in recent years in discovering and producing the work of young British dramatists.

ROYAL COURT BOOKSHOP

The bookshop offers a wide range of playtexts, theatre books, screenplays and art-house videos with over 1,000 titles.

Located in the downstairs BAR AND FOOD area, the bookshop is open Monday to Saturday, afternoons and evenings.

Many of the Royal Court Theatre playtexts are available for just £2 including the plays in the current season and recent works by Conor McPherson, Martin Crimp, Sarah Kane, David Mamet, Phyllis Nagy, Gary Mitchell, Marina Carr, Martin McDonagh, Ayub Khan-Din, Jim Cartwright and Rebecca Prichard. We offer a 10% reduction to students on a range of titles.

Further information : 020 7565 5024

THE FORCE OF CHANGE

To Chuck Mitchell

Characters

CAROLINE PATTERSON, *35, Detective Sergeant, married with two children*
MARK SIMPSON, *37, Detective Sergeant, single*
BILL BYRNE, *57, Detective Constable, married with children and grandchildren*
DAVID DAVIS, *30, Detective Constable, single*
STANLEY BROWN, *28, single of no fixed abode. Accused of membership of the UDA and directing terrorism*
RABBIT – ROBERT MONTGOMERY, *19, petty criminal, mainly joyriding*

The entire play takes place in two interview rooms and a corridor.

Note

Detectives wear suits and are unarmed. Stanley Brown is wearing his own casual clothes and Robert Montgomery is wearing a boiler suit and plimsolls supplied by the RUC as his clothes are required for tests.

The names of characters and places, including police stations, divisions and departments of as well as ranks, are merely suggestions; these can be altered for reasons of sensitivity or security. Dates may also be changed, if thought beneficial.

ACT ONE

Interview Room A

BILL *enters the interview room and checks that the furniture and equipment are arranged properly.* BILL *loads two tapes into the tape recorder.* BILL *leaves the room.* CAROLINE *enters the corridor as he does so.*

Corridor

CAROLINE. You're in early today.

BILL. I'm always in early.

CAROLINE. No you're not. See, if you were I would notice because I *am* actually always in early. (*Pause.*) Unless you come in early and hide somewhere. Is that what you do?

BILL. If you must know I'm in *particularly* early today because I thought you would have *appreciated* an early start given the fact that there is only now five hours before we have to let Stanley Brown go.

CAROLINE. I didn't realise you were so keen. Is that something else you hide?

BILL. I'll get the files.

BILL, *slightly annoyed, walks casually away.* CAROLINE *takes out her mobile phone and dials.*

CAROLINE ((*her daughter answers the phone*). Hello, why are you not at school? (*Pause.*) Honey, that's no excuse I left all your swimming gear out for you. (*Pause.*) Yes. Never mind, where's your Daddy? No, there's nothing wrong, go and get him for me.

CAROLINE *waits until her husband comes to the phone. As* CAROLINE *waits for her husband to come to the phone she moves through and checks Interview Room B. It is empty and so she returns to Interview Room A.*

Interview Room A

CAROLINE. No no. Definitely not. See I knew as soon as I was out the door he would do that. I did not say Henry could go on the trip. What I said was that you and I would discuss it at some point . . . *(She is interrupted, listens.)* . . . Whenever? Don't start . . . I said whenever . . . Whenever I get home. Of course he would say that I would say that because that is what I'm saying. Darling, listen to me, if you think it's all right for him to go let him go, if you don't think it's all right for him to go then he's not going. How's that? *(Listens.)* Me, I don't mind. I was all for him going until now. No, if he's messing me about then I think the appropriate punishment is that I leave it up to you to decide. *(Interrupted again.)* That's not what I mean.

BILL *re-enters the room carrying files.* CAROLINE *signals that they should be set on the desk beside her and that* BILL *should then leave and give her two minutes before returning again.* BILL *leaves.*

CAROLINE. I didn't say that it was too dangerous for him to go. *(Takes file from top of pile and sets it to the side. Takes second file and opens it.)* I said that you would think, *(Corrects herself.)* that you might think that it was too dangerous for him to go. *(Begins to flick through the pages of the file.)* Honey . . . Why don't you decide . . . *(Becomes interested in a page and reads it.)* . . . and whatever you decide . . . No I'm not shirking my responsibilities at all . . . No I'm not putting it all on you I . . . What I'm saying is, I don't care either way. *(Holds the phone away from her ear and reads more.)* If you decide no but you'd rather I told him, then I'll do it, I'll tell him and I'll tell him why. *(He talks.)* OK I won't tell him why but I will tell him if you don't want to be the bad guy.

MARK *enters the room carrying a cup of tea in one hand and a 'big thick file' in the other.*

CAROLINE. Honey, look the Inspector's just come in I got to go. I'll talk to you later. *(After thought.)* Tell Maggie next time she forgets something she's on her own, no more of this running back and forth. Love you, bye.

CAROLINE *hangs up and tosses the phone to the side.*

MARK (*jokes*). I got promoted and nobody told me. Wait 'til the folks hear about this.

CAROLINE. You're very funny.

MARK. What? (*Acts unsure that he knows what she means.*) Don't tell me I didn't get promoted and that you were just lying to whoever it was on the other end of that phone? That's dishonest.

CAROLINE. Why have you only one cup with you?

MARK (*playing a defendant*). This is actually your tea. I was bringing this . . . I was walking by earlier and I heard a noise and I saw . . .

CAROLINE. What noise?

MARK *moves to the desk and sets the cup down.*

MARK. Take the tea.

CAROLINE. Have you drunk out of this cup?

MARK. No. Why would I do that?

It is obviously not to her taste.

CAROLINE. There's sugar in this.

MARK. You stopped taking sugar?

CAROLINE. I never took sugar.

MARK. Are you lying to me again?

CAROLINE (*playfully*). Take your tea back.

MARK (*seriously*). Do you want me to get you a cup?

CAROLINE. No, I want you to tell me why everybody is in early today.

MARK. What can I say, we're an enthusiastic bunch.

CAROLINE. Is it to do with me?

MARK. Why would it be to do with you?

CAROLINE. Time is up today. And I'm just getting this feeling that people are gathering like . . . vultures to see me fail.

MARK. No, I don't think there's a reason like that. Just co-incidence.

CAROLINE. Last time I got promoted I had to go through months of them scrutinising every thing I did.

MARK. Them?

CAROLINE. My colleagues. (*Pause*.) If something went wrong, which it usually does, I mean we've all had those experiences but the difference with me was that they would suddenly talk about it, always as though it was my fault and . . . it was as if they wanted it broadcast to the world to prove their theory that the only reason I got promoted was . . .

MARK. . . . because in the minds of that promotion board you were the best man for the job. (*Realises the slip*.) Did I say man there? I did, didn't I?

CAROLINE (*ignoring the slip*). I just have this feeling that they've changed their tactics and they think that by reporting my little mistakes before the Inspector makes his recommendation will . . . you know . . .

MARK. I think you're maybe just getting a little bit paranoid.

CAROLINE. That wouldn't be hard.

MARK. Well answer me this, what benefit is it to anybody here who may or may not like you to have the Inspector not recommend you for promotion? I mean surely that is the best way to get rid of you. I don't mean it like that but if you think about it.

CAROLINE. They don't want to get rid of me they want to stop me.

MARK. I don't think so.

CAROLINE. I'm only saying that's how it feels.

MARK. The Inspector is probably the only person really watching you. As he would watch anybody he was doing a report on. He's got what, two days left?

CAROLINE. Two days before he has to send it yes.

MARK. I don't blame you for being nervous, but that's all it is. Nerves. Totally understandable.

CAROLINE. Maybe you're right.

MARK. I usually am. How's it going anyway?

CAROLINE. Not good.

MARK. Has he spoken yet?

CAROLINE. Oh no.

MARK. I hate that. You just sit in these rooms with these bastards saying nothing all day. (*Pause.*) Tell me, do you think the UDA actually hold little evening classes in some pub somewhere where they teach these guys how to fuck us off? (*Acts UDA leader.*) In an interview situation with our local constabulary an officer will attempt to get as much information from you as possible. Remember at all times that anything you say may be used in evidence against you. He will bribe you, browbeat you, threaten you and bore you to a point where in a moment of weakness or retaliation you might just slip up and say something. And although you might think you have told him nothing, you may have, in actual fact, implicated yourself or others in a serious crime and thereby jeopardise an ongoing or future operation. In order to avoid compromising yourself or others it is advised that you say nothing, nothing at all, ever.

CAROLINE. Surely, they would say, 'Never. No. Never.'

BILL *enters the room as she speaks. This little 'act' makes* BILL *suspicious of what they were talking about.*

CAROLINE (*deliberately changing the subject*). How's Daphne?

MARK. Debbie?

CAROLINE. Debbie? Did I get that name wrong or are you trying to tell me that you've got another new woman?

MARK. You got the name wrong. And she's fine.

CAROLINE. Thank God for that. I hate the 'getting to know your colleague's partner' routine.

MARK. Husbands can be dead boring to get to know too.

CAROLINE *feigns emotional hurt.*

BILL. What time did you want to start today?

CAROLINE. Five minutes.

MARK. How's Bill?

BILL. Bill's fine.

> *Pause.* BILL *sits in his chair at the table.* MARK *watches him.*

MARK. Mark's fine too. Thanks for asking.

BILL. Who brought the tea?

MARK. Me, why do you want a cup?

BILL. Does the Pope shit in the woods?

> BILL *finds himself funny.* MARK *looks at* CAROLINE *puzzled.* BILL *tries to explain himself.*

BILL. I've been dying to say that since I heard a guy in the pub saying it on Saturday night.

CAROLINE. But it doesn't make sense, Bill.

MARK. What pub was this?

BILL. It does make sense. It's a combination of, you know, does a bear . . .

CAROLINE. We know what it was a combination of.

MARK (*repeats with a more serious tone*). What pub was this?

BILL. Just my pub . . . my local pub.

MARK. And that would be where?

BILL. Well if it's my local then it would be near where I live.

CAROLINE. Bill, why don't you go and get yourself a cup of tea and then we can have a chat before bringing Muteman in?

> BILL *waits, glaring at* MARK *and thinking.* BILL *obviously doesn't want to go and get the tea.* BILL *resents being ordered to do so, particularly by a woman.* BILL *waits longer than usual.*

CAROLINE. Bill?

> BILL *throws a few disapproving looks around the room before getting up and walking slowly out again.*

MARK. He's in good form.

CAROLINE. Is it men's time of the month or something? Harry's on the phone every two minutes with this problem or that problem. Wee Henry's throwing major tantrums all morning because 'We' won't let him go away with the school. Then, I come in here to be greeted by Inspector Grumpy and Whining Bill Hickcock there.

MARK. I'm in a good mood.

CAROLINE. Oh, well then everything's fine. Great, so long as you're in a good mood.

Silence.

MARK. Here's something that might cheer you up. The TACT boys are sending over one Robert Montgomery. His nickname is Rabbit, he's a joyrider or he used to be.

CAROLINE *takes the file and begins to flick through it.* CAROLINE *finds the page with details of interest and reads it.*

CAROLINE. Used to be?

MARK. We've been told that he's recently been recruited by Stanley Brown for the UDA.

CAROLINE. Everything on his record seems to be joyriding related.

MARK. That's my problem. I know I can make this mutt talk but how soon . . . You know what I mean . . . Maybe you should think about releasing Brown until we get something. You should keep some time in reserve for later.

CAROLINE. I've enough time for two blasts today, either side of lunch. That ought to do it.

Silence.

MARK. What are you doing for lunch?

CAROLINE. Don't know yet.

MARK. What do you say we go to a restaurant instead of the canteen again? It could be your last chance to recharge your batteries for the final onslaught.

CAROLINE. Sounds excellent, but I think I'll have to pass. Maybe just grab something quick.

MARK *considers his options and watches* CAROLINE.

MARK (*hesitates*). What about a drink after work?

CAROLINE. Why are you not going straight home?

MARK. Because I'd rather go for a drink with you.

CAROLINE. Don't give me that, I've met Daphne, (*Corrects herself, quickly.*) Debbie. And I know you, so there's no way you could possibly want to drink with me instead of . . . you know.

MARK. Instead of what?

CAROLINE. Instead of spending time with your partner.

MARK. You're my partner sometimes.

CAROLINE. I'm your work partner. She's your girlfriend partner.

MARK. Why not just say girlfriend then?

CAROLINE. Because she doesn't like being called 'girlfriend'.

MARK. I call her girlfriend all the time. (*Thinking quickly.*) When did she say this?

CAROLINE. It doesn't matter, but now you know not to call her it anymore. (*Pauses, allowing* MARK *time to think.*) So, what's the real reason.

MARK. It's Tuesday. She goes to night school.

CAROLINE. You never told me that.

MARK. Well, it's a bit embarrassing. And don't be saying anything to her. I don't know if this is one of those 'secrets between us' things or not.

CAROLINE. I won't.

MARK. Unless she says something to you. Like if she mentions it first . . .

CAROLINE. What's she doing?

MARK. A Business course.

CAROLINE. She can't have brains too.

MARK. Well this is it. She has a thing about that.

CAROLINE. The dumb blonde thing? (*Jokingly.*) I know I get it all the time. You should tell her that's just a man thing or a jealous bitch thing.

MARK. What about that drink?

CAROLINE. I don't know what's going to happen today.

MARK. Look at it like this, if you get a result we can go celebrate and if you don't then we can go commiserate.

CAROLINE (*considers*). Can I get back to you?

MARK. Don't leave it too late, I might get a better offer.

CAROLINE. Take my advice, head off early, go shopping and then home . . .

MARK. Shopping for what?

CAROLINE. That's the punch line, hear me out. Go home, make her favourite meal, with her favourite wine, put on her favourite suit add a little music a few candles and after dinner you get down on one knee and give her the surprise.

MARK. I did that on Sunday.

CAROLINE. You got engaged on Sunday?

MARK. No, we had great sex.

CAROLINE. Get out! Take your stinking sugary tea and get out.

MARK *takes the file.*

CAROLINE. Could you get Bill to make a copy of that?

MARK. I don't think he would appreciate that.

CAROLINE. Get the Custody Sergeant to do it, we get on like that.

Gestures that they are best friends.

MARK. What's her name then?

CAROLINE. Very funny.

MARK. What is it? Her first name?

CAROLINE. She wouldn't have to copy the whole thing, just bits. Be a darling and sort it out for me, you know you want to.

MARK *laughs as he leaves the room.* CAROLINE *sits and flicks through her own files, stops at a particular one and begins to browse.*

Interview Room B

MARK *enters Interview Room B and begins to go through*
RABBIT's *file, taking out sections to photocopy. Shortly after,*
DAVID *enters.*

DAVID. Speedy Gonzales has arrived, Mark.

MARK. Rabbit.

DAVID. Sorry?

MARK. He likes to be called Rabbit.

DAVID. Why would anyone like to be called Rabbit?

MARK. What was your nickname in school?

DAVID. I didn't have one.

MARK. What about University?

DAVID. I've never had a nickname.

MARK. Not even Dave or Davy?

DAVID. No. (*Losing interest.*) Is this Montgomery's file?

MARK. Have you ever had a girlfriend who gave you a pet
    name?

DAVID (*browsing through the first section that* MARK *has
    separated*). Are these the good bits?

MARK. There's no good bits in here. I'm just trying to find
    bits that might help Caroline out with Stanley Brown.

DAVID. Why can she not do it?

MARK. We've only got one file mate.

DAVID. Get a copy.

MARK. Well if you had seen the form Bill was in you would . . .

DAVID. Give me the file.

MARK. What are you going to do?

DAVID. I'm going to get it copied.

MARK. That's very decent of you.

DAVID. Don't thank me, thank Judy.

MARK. You'll never get Judy to copy that lot.

DAVID. People skills.

MARK. Well you do that. I'm going to take a piss and think of a good nickname for you.

DAVID. Great.

DAVID *is about to leave but hesitates at the door.*

DAVID. Why not just think of a good reason for us to go in and have a go at Stanley Brown. You know we could break him in five minutes.

MARK. It's not our case.

DAVID. She's fucking it up. Brown's going to walk.

They leave.

Interview Room A

Eventually BILL *returns with two steaming polystyrene cups of tea.*

BILL. Is it Ok for me to come in now that lover boy's gone?

CAROLINE. Lover boy? I didn't know you guys had pet names for each other, when did that start?

BILL. Funny.

CAROLINE. Have I got one?

BILL *smiles at the thought of a name or two then sits.* CAROLINE *reads.* BILL *watches* CAROLINE *reading and then interrupts.*

BILL. What's the plan?

CAROLINE. Same as yesterday.

BILL. Fill me in. What was the plan yesterday?

CAROLINE. We have to wear him down.

BILL. What way today?

CAROLINE. I'm reading.

CAROLINE *returns to the file.* BILL *continues to watch her, then interrupts again, obviously agitated.*

BILL. It's just that I'd like to know. You see yesterday I thought you were the good cop and I was the bad cop but then you started yelling and screaming and . . .

CAROLINE. Don't go all 'old school' on me Bill.

BILL. I'm trying to be professional.

CAROLINE. Then follow my lead.

BILL. I've been trying to do that but you go all over the place. I don't know what I'm supposed to be following.

CAROLINE. That's the point Bill. You see if you don't know then Mr Muteman won't know either and that could give us the edge we need. (*Pauses to watch if the idea sinks in to* BILL. *It doesn't.*) Improvise Bill.

BILL. I'd rather we had a plan.

CAROLINE. We do have a plan.

BILL. I spoke to the Inspector . . .

CAROLINE. You what?

BILL. I wanted a second opinion because I'm uncomfortable –

CAROLINE. A *second* opinion?

BILL. – with your style . . .

CAROLINE. What was the first opinion Bill?

BILL. I can't work the way you do.

CAROLINE. Is this a woman thing?

BILL *shakes his head.*

CAROLINE. If you can't work with me why don't you put in for a transfer?

BILL. I like it here.

CAROLINE. Well then cope with it.

BILL. I also told the Inspector, just so as you know . . .

CAROLINE. Yes?

BILL. That I feel uncomfortable having to leave the room every five minutes when your husband rings.

CAROLINE. I don't believe you.

BILL. No offence, I was only trying to clear the air.

CAROLINE. No you weren't. If you were only trying to clear the air you would've told me first. And my husband doesn't ring every five minutes.

BILL. That's not the point.

CAROLINE. That's a gross exaggeration. You're trying to paint a darker picture of our . . . What about when your friends ring you? Have you ever heard me complaining about that?

BILL. I don't order you out of the room.

CAROLINE. If someone rang you in here then I would leave the room out of courtesy.

BILL. Nobody can ring me in this room. I always switch mine off and let them leave a message.

CAROLINE *stands and begins to pace.* BILL *watches her.* CAROLINE *continually shakes her head in disbelief, takes a deep breath and composes herself.*

CAROLINE. I'll get a pager. (*Pauses.*) And if it rings I'll leave the room, how's that?

BILL. Whatever you want.

CAROLINE. Look Bill. If we don't work this little problem out between ourselves it will end up on both our records.

BILL *disregards this statement.*

CAROLINE. Doesn't that mean anything to you?

BILL. I'm not going anywhere.

CAROLINE. You can still go down the ladder, Bill.

BILL *smiles.* CAROLINE *glares at him, sips her tea and returns to the file.* BILL *waits. Eventually,* CAROLINE *seems to have found something interesting on the page in front of her.* CAROLINE *considers her options for a moment while tapping her pen on the page and then stands.*

CAROLINE. Let's wake Muteman up.

CAROLINE *walks out of the room.* BILL *finishes his tea and then disposes of the polystyrene cup in the bin.* BILL *checks his pockets and produces his cigarettes, he checks he has 'enough to do' and replaces them in his pocket.*

CAROLINE *returns carrying two notebooks, one new and one used and tapes.*

CAROLINE. Have you not got him yet?

BILL. I'll get him now.

BILL *leaves the room slowly.* CAROLINE *begins to log the tapes, checking the tape that's in the recorder and noting a number in her book.* CAROLINE *sits and makes notes and tips to herself.* BILL *returns with* STANLEY BROWN *(Muteman).*

CAROLINE. Come in Mr Brown. Take a seat and make yourself comfortable.

STANLEY *walks matter-of-factly to his seat and sits.* BILL *closes the door and takes his seat.* CAROLINE *stares at* STANLEY.

CAROLINE. I hope you had a pleasant night's sleep here in our humble establishment. I know the custody sergeant hates to deal with complaints. Have you got any complaints Mr Brown? They don't have to be verbal, I can get you a notebook and a pen if you want. (*Pause.*) No? Good.

STANLEY *looks at* BILL.

CAROLINE. Don't look at him, look at me Mr Brown. Oh, (*Cringes.*) there's that name again. Mr Brown. No matter how often I say it I just can't get used to it. It's like that film, what was it . . . ah . . . what do you call that film, Bill?

BILL. Don't know.

CAROLINE. You must know it. Cops and robbers and . . .

BILL. That narrows it down.

BILL *smiles at* STANLEY.

CAROLINE. English actor plays the Undercover Cop.

BILL *shakes his head.* CAROLINE *looks to* STANLEY *as if asking him.*

CAROLINE. They all meet in a warehouse. Tim Roth? Sean Penn? No his brother, the fat one. No? It was a great movie. They have a scene where they're all gathered to get code names for this job they have to do but this one guy doesn't like his name. Mr Brown. (*Acts Tarantino.*) Mr Brown that's a bit like Mr Shit.

CAROLINE *glares at* STANLEY.

CAROLINE. Did he base that scene on the UDA? (*To* BILL.) What do you think Bill? Do you remember the UDA had those code names? Mr White, Mr Black.

BILL (*corrects* CAROLINE). Colonel White, Captain Black.

CAROLINE. Oh yeah. Colonel White, Captain Black, Captain Orange of course . . . (*Interrupts herself.*) Did they have a Captain Pink? (*No answer.*) What about Captain Scarlet? (*Does the theme tune from Captain Scarlet.*) Or Captain Caveman? (*This is shouted in true 'Captain Caveman' style.*) Were they in the UDA? (*Still no answer.*) Do you know what I liked most of all about that movie? The Cops won in the end. All the criminals got killed. If only life was like that.

CAROLINE *smiles, then paces, unaware that she has annoyed* BILL *more than* STANLEY.

CAROLINE. Does the UDA still have code names, Mr Brown? Do you have a code name? (*Pause.*) Or a nickname? (*Pretends to think.*) Browner, the Brownman, Browney, Brown Boy? No, they're awful names. What do you prefer to be called? Stanley? Stan the Man? Stanney? Stancer, Stanno?

BILL *stands and walks to the table.* CAROLINE *sees this.*

BILL. Will I start recording?

CAROLINE. Ask him.

BILL. I'm asking you.

CAROLINE (*to* STANLEY). Have you something to say to me, Mr Brown?

CAROLINE *waits.*

CAROLINE (*to* BILL). Go and get some cigarettes and check with the Custody Sergeant to see if Stanley's allowed a cup of tea or not. Do you like tea, Stanley?

No response.

CAROLINE. Go Bill and then we'll start.

BILL *looks to* STANLEY.

BILL. Judy's on today, she won't allow tea unless I say it's for me. (*To* STANLEY.) Do you want me to say it's for me?

STANLEY *looks at* BILL. BILL *watches, expecting a response.* STANLEY *looks away and* CAROLINE *gestures with her head that* BILL *should go.*

BILL. I'm a bit uncomfortable about leaving you alone.

CAROLINE. I'm not alone, I've got Chatterbox here for company.

BILL *leaves.* CAROLINE *relaxes.*

CAROLINE. What kind of movies do you like, Stanley?

STANLEY *looks at* CAROLINE *and then the door.*

CAROLINE. Westerns? No, I bet you like a good weepy. Am I right?

STANLEY *looks back at* CAROLINE *and then the floor.*

CAROLINE. Don't be predictable and tell me that you prefer Gangster movies. (*Waits.*) Maybe genre isn't important to you. Tell me, which do you prefer, big budget Hollywood or low budget European? I know you don't like Asian with all that dancing and singing. Chinese, a bit of Kung Fu? You're going to be predictable again and say you only like British movies, aren't you? And you hate Irish ones. Am I right?

CAROLINE *paces.*

CAROLINE. I'm not that keen on them myself. They always make the Irish out to be stupid or funny and drunk. But then again you don't think of yourself as Irish, do you? (STANLEY *glares at* CAROLINE *and then looks away.* CAROLINE *thinks about his reaction.*) See that look on your face I could've predicted that. That should be your code name, Mr Predictable. Do you know what else I can predict? Sooner or later you're going to make a mistake and when you do I'm going to be here and you're going to want to talk to me so much but do you know what I'm going to do? (*Pauses as though waiting for an answer.*) No you don't, I don't even know what I'm going to do then. Maybe I'll be all vengeful and not talk back or maybe I'll be so pleased at having you crawl and beg and plead that I will talk. Don't know. That's the difference between us. That's maybe why I prefer suspense movies like Hitchcock. Psycho, do you remember that? Horror movies. Do you like Horror movies? No? What about Porno? Do you like Porno Stanley or do you find it repulsive, degrading to women and all that?

As she speaks, CAROLINE *picks up the top file and opens it. Pretends to browse through it.*

CAROLINE. Jackie Phillips liked Porno, Stanley? I know because I was in the process of investigating him when four men took him out of his house, set it on fire and then shot him in the knees. They probably saw it as part of their crusade against Pornography or part of their defence of the Protestant community in general. Either way it didn't work. See Stanley thanks to those idiots Jackie Phillips is still free and clean. He's still out there, he might have a limp but he's still around, still free to start all over again only next time he'll be more careful and a lot harder to catch. (*Pause.*) The tape's not on, just between me and you. Was that your idea?

CAROLINE *places the Phillips file to the side and picks up the second file.*

CAROLINE. Mrs Jennifer Walsh. Nice woman. Her first statement was all about you. She saw you, according to this version, her original statement, she saw you shoot poor Jackie Phillips in both knees. But she made this statement before someone paid her a visit and told her all about what the evil Jackie Phillips was doing. (*Pause.*) Did you pay her or threaten her? You don't have to say, I'm just curious.

CAROLINE *places the Walsh file to the side on top of the Phillips file and takes the third.*

CAROLINE. Mr Henry Walker. Owns Walkers Off-licence. Apparently you threatened him. (*Reads a bit.*) No, you sent your goons first. Were they just the usual collectors or did you bring them in specially? You're going to have to get new ones because according to this you had to go and see Mr Henry Walker yourself. Strange because as soon as we arrested you he gave us a second statement saying that he had (*As if reading.*) misunderstood your conversation. Then after we released you he even gave us a third statement claiming that this misunderstanding wasn't even with you but actually someone entirely different. Someone he couldn't even describe to us. Is this all just coincidence?

CAROLINE *places the Walker file on top of the Walsh file and picks up the fourth.*

CAROLINE. This is my favourite. Statement One, 2nd of March. (*Reads.*) I, Mr Thomas Lawrence, was doing my shopping as normal on the 1st of March when I called in to Walkers Off-licence for some cigarettes. I usually get them somewhere else because as I'm not a drinking man I normally don't go into the off-licence but on this day I was passing and I had forgotten my cigarettes so I just ended up going into Walkers, just for cigarettes not drink. My wife doesn't drink either and she doesn't like me to drink and I don't anyway. The door was jammed over and a young man was standing just inside. I thought this was peculiar but when I asked the young man to help me by moving out of the way of the door and opening it he told me to 'F' off and called me names. I was quite frightened and scared because I'm old and I'm not well. Twenty years ago maybe I would have done something but today I had taken a wee twinge or two. So I wasn't going to take this wee lad on. Wee lad as in young lad because he was actually quite tall. But I did look over his shoulder and saw (*Emphasises the words.*) quite clearly Stanley Brown pressing a small revolver against the side of Henry Walker's head. (*Stops reading and looks at STANLEY.*) Tut, tut Stanley. (*Continues.*) I fooled the big wee lad into thinking I had seen nothing by diverting my glance quickly and strolling away as though everything was normal. When I got home and told my wife she asked me . . . (*To STANLEY.*) it actually says sent me and then it has a line through it . . . anyway (*Pause.*) she asked me to come straight down here and report it. Not for any reward or anything because there aren't any rewards for things like this, sure there aren't? (*Pause.*) Statement Two. This one is dated 6th of March. I, Thomas Lawrence, was passing the Walker's off-licence on the 1st of March when I realised I had to get some cigarettes. I went in and bought them and the whole time I was there I saw nothing out of the ordinary and came straight home. I am not well though and sometimes I think I see things that I don't actually see.

CAROLINE *stops reading and glares at* STANLEY.

CAROLINE. Thomas Lawrence is sixty-eight, Stanley. Did you press your revolver to the side of his head? (*Pause.*) See this is what really sickens me about you and people like you. You actually believe that this makes you a hero, don't you? Threatening old men, intimidating old women, extorting money from ordinary decent people who are just trying to make a living. Don't get me wrong I'm no Nationalist sympathiser. In fact, once upon a time the Ulster Defence Association would have been an organisation people like myself might have had a little time for, whilst not being fully supportive at least we would have had some sympathy or understanding of their motivations. An organisation established solely with one aim to serve and protect the Unionist population of Northern Ireland. Nothing too much wrong with that but that was the seventies and things were different then. What has this great Protestant organisation become? A bunch of half wit criminals like you. Last I heard they were even using Joyriders.

STANLEY *stops smiling.*

Silence.

CAROLINE. Maybe I'm wrong. Maybe I'm barking up the wrong tree. Maybe you're not the bad guy here. Maybe you're not responsible for recruitment. What do you say? (*Pause.*) Do you pick the teams for these crimes, do you recruit the next batch of proud defenders of Ulster or are you just an innocent pawn here? Maybe that's someone else's department, maybe all you do is threaten people, sorry, collect money. Which one is it? I mean I think we can safely say that you're not the hero of the hour. You're not the good guy on the white horse. In fact you're more like the shit the white horse drops behind as it walks. (*Pause.*) It's up to you, you tell me. Are you the dog's bollocks or are you the dog's ass hole?

Sustained silence.

BILL *returns.*

CAROLINE (*as though mid-conversation with* STANLEY). I know what you're saying but you don't have to go on and on about it.

BILL. What do you mean?

CAROLINE. I'm glad you're back. He was doing my head in with his constant ranting.

BILL *places a cup of water in front of* STANLEY.

CAROLINE. She wouldn't allow the tea then?

BILL. I told you she wouldn't. But she said this is for you.

BILL *gives* CAROLINE *the file Judy copied for* DAVID.

CAROLINE. She's not picking on you Stanley. She has this thing, to some people tea is a refreshment but to others it can be a lethal weapon. Personally, I don't think it tastes that bad at all.

CAROLINE *moves to the tape recorder and presses record.*

CAROLINE. This interview is being tape recorded. The interview is being conducted in an interview room at Antrim Road Police Station. I am Detective Sergeant Patterson attached to Antrim Road Police Station. The other officer present is Detective Constable Byrne also attached to Castlereagh Police Station. The date is May 5th 2000 and the time is (*Checks watch.*) 09.01. (*Notes time on seal of tape.*) Recommencing interview with Stanley Brown. There is no other person present.

BILL *leaves a cigarette and lighter on the table for* STANLEY. CAROLINE *presses pause.*

CAROLINE. Don't leave the lighter on the table.

BILL. What?

CAROLINE. He's a dangerous criminal.

BILL. He's not going to do anything with it.

CAROLINE. Give him a light but keep the lighter.

BILL *offers to light the cigarette.* STANLEY *refuses the offer.*

BILL. Right.

BILL *looks to* CAROLINE *for direction.* CAROLINE *presses record again.*

CAROLINE. You are reminded that you have the right to independent legal advice. You may at any time consult or communicate privately, either in person, in writing or on the telephone, with a solicitor. Do you want to speak to a solicitor? (*Pause.*) I also remind you that you do not have to say anything, but I must caution you that if you do not mention when questioned something which you later rely on in court, it may harm your defence. If you do say anything it may be given in evidence.

CAROLINE *makes her way to the table.*

CAROLINE. Did you Stanley Brown threaten or intimidate in any way Mr Thomas Lawrence?

BILL. Let the record show that the accused made no gesture, nor did he make any attempt to deny the accusation.

CAROLINE. Did you Stanley Brown actively encourage or direct or request that anyone known to you should threaten or intimidate in any way Mr Thomas Lawrence?

BILL. Let the record show that the accused made no gesture, nor did he make any attempt to deny the accusation.

STANLEY *takes a drink of water.*

CAROLINE. Did you Stanley Brown threaten or intimidate in anyway Mr Harold Walker?

BILL. Let the record show that the accused made no gesture, nor did he make any attempt to deny the accusation.

CAROLINE. Did you Stanley Brown extort money from any person working in Walkers Off-licence?

BILL. Let the record show that the accused made no gesture, nor did he make any attempt to deny the accusation.

Pause.

CAROLINE. Did you Stanley Brown direct Robert Montgomery, aka Rabbit, to steal a BMW for the UDA?

BILL. Let the record show that the accused made no gesture, nor did he make any attempt to deny the accusation.

CAROLINE. Do you Stanley Brown know who did direct Robert Montgomery to steal a BMW?

BILL. Let the record show that the accused made no gesture.

CAROLINE *suddenly stands and walks away.* STANLEY *watches.* CAROLINE *turns to face him.* STANLEY *smiles.*

CAROLINE (*shouts at* STANLEY). Shut the fuck up.

CAROLINE *goes to the table and takes the cigarettes and the water away from* STANLEY.

CAROLINE. You can't have these.

STANLEY *stops smiling.*

CAROLINE. You can't have another thing today.

BILL. Let the record show that Detective Patterson has taken the cigarette and cup of water away from the accused.

CAROLINE *stands staring at* BILL. CAROLINE *moves to the tape recorder.*

CAROLINE (*rhymes off quickly*). Before I switch off the tape recorder do you wish to add anything further or to clarify any point or anything you have told me? Interview suspended.

CAROLINE *presses stop on the tape recorder.*

BILL. What are you doing?

CAROLINE. I need a break. He has the kind of voice that just goes right through you.

CAROLINE *walks out of the room.* BILL *looks at* STANLEY *for a moment before offering him a cigarette.* STANLEY *takes the cigarette.*

Interview Room B

MARK *is in the process of interviewing* RABBIT MONTGOMERY. MARK *is being assisted by Detective Constable* DAVID DAVIS. DAVID *has a cup of tea.*

MARK. Do you know who we have next door?

RABBIT *shakes his head.*

MARK. Stanley Brown.

Pause.

MARK. Do you know him?

RABBIT. Stocky fella, black hair. Tattoos on both arms. (*Waits for* MARK *to nod.*) Never heard of him.

RABBIT *laughs at his own joke.*

DAVID. Comedian?

MARK. That's very good. I'm glad you can see the funny side of all this. I can't. I find stealing a car, racing through busy streets endangering life and evading the Police a very serious business indeed. (*Pause.*) If that is in fact what was really going on.

DAVID. Word on the street is that Stanley Brown recommended you to the local UDA chief. Do you remember him now?

RABBIT. I'm not in the UDA.

MARK. No?

MARK *picks up the only file on the desk and opens it.*

MARK (*jokingly to* DAVID). This must be all wrong, David. Can we get this checked out?

DAVID (*playing* MARK's *game*). I don't think that's necessary.

MARK. Why not?

DAVID. He's just admitted it, hasn't he?

MARK. How do you mean?

DAVID. Well, it's a well known fact that any kid who says he's in the UDA in actual fact isn't.

MARK. Because the kid who says he is in the UDA would only be bragging or trying to play the big man?

DAVID. Yeah. So if that's true then surely any kid who says he isn't in the UDA, in actual fact must be.

MARK. I see what you mean. That's clever.

DAVID. They're smart boys.

MARK. What do you say to that, Rabbit?

RABBIT. That's bullshit. I said I'm not in the UDA and that's what it means.

MARK. Can you prove it?

RABBIT. I don't have to prove anything. This isn't France you know.

MARK (*to* DAVID, *surprised*). This boy knows his stuff. I think we're in trouble here.

DAVID. That's obviously why Stanley recommended him.

MARK. Maybe. (*Pause.*) Is that what you think Rabbit?

Pause. There is no reaction from RABBIT.

MARK. Do you think Stanley picked you for your smarts? I mean I think we can safely say it wasn't for your looks.

Pause.

MARK. The thing that troubles me about that theory is this though. If they picked you for your smarts why did they allow you to go Joyriding? I mean they must've known that you're prone to a little bit of car theft. Your record reeks of it.

DAVID. Maybe they thought of his record in a different way. Like he holds the record for the longest joyride or the fastest joyride.

MARK (*to* DAVID). Maybe.

DAVID. It is such a waste of talent.

MARK. It is. I agree totally.

DAVID. Reginald, from traffic, told me this morning that he had to be at his very best to catch him.

MARK. Reginald, the Knight Rider, said that (*Little hesitation.*) about this mutt? He's our number one pursuer, Rabbit. How do you feel about that?

RABBIT. He got fucking lucky.

DAVID. He said that.

MARK. You must be good son.

RABBIT. I'm the best.

DAVID. Brings me back to my point, it's such a waste of talent.

MARK. Why don't you put these skills to a more productive use?

Pause. There is no reaction from RABBIT.

DAVID. Too many options maybe. That can happen when a person is multi-talented. Ultimately they wind up a Jack of all trades and master of none.

MARK. Is that it?

DAVID. If I had to pick between Rally Driver or Formula One or a life in show business it would tear at me. I mean how could you give any of them up?

MARK. Is that what you're going through, Rabbit?

RABBIT. You're the fucking comedy duo, you two. Not me.

MARK. I'm being serious, Rabbit. You see this. (*Holds the file towards* RABBIT.) This is one of the, what we call, big fat files. And do you know the thing about big fat files? (*To* DAVID.) Tell him.

DAVID. It shows an attitude of carelessness, some might think of as amateurish but others might say it shows a lack of interest.

MARK. We think that people who continually break the law, in a small and similar way, like all this stuff in here. It's almost habitual. These people aren't serious about what they do. Their hearts aren't in it. And to be honest these people don't really interest us.

MARK *tosses* RABBIT*'s file into the bin.* RABBIT *watches this, almost insulted.*

MARK. What we're after are the small thin files.

DAVID *nods at* RABBIT.

MARK. Stanley Brown's file is so thin it's unbelievable. (*To* DAVID.) What's it like, David?

DAVID *gestures with his fingers that* STANLEY BROWN*'s file is wafer thin.*

MARK. I'm telling you all this so as you know where you stand. We're not out to get you.

DAVID. If we were you'd be locked up already.

MARK. The key would be long gone.

Pause.

MARK. We're here to help you.

DAVID. Think of it as rehabilitation.

MARK. As I'm sure you're aware from your past stays in Young Offender Centres and indeed your recent court appearances, rehabilitation is becoming more and more part of our service.

DAVID. Arresting, prosecuting and locking you away hasn't exactly proved fruitful for you or the community now has it, Rabbit?

MARK. See what we're saying. I'm not going to waste our time or the taxpayer's money going down that road again. No. I want to help you Rabbit. It's up to you whether or not you want to be helped.

RABBIT. I'm a bit confused. Which one of yous is playing the Good Cop?

DAVID. We're not playing anything.

MARK. Are you thirsty? Do you want a wee cup of tea or something?

DAVID. I'll get it.

MARK. No. I'll get it.

DAVID. I don't mind honestly, you sit down. (*To* RABBIT.) Coffee?

MARK. Hot Chocolate?

DAVID. Coke?

MARK. Sprite?

DAVID. 7 Up?

DAVID *and* MARK. Same thing.

DAVID. Fanta?

MARK. Ribena?

DAVID. Squash?

MARK. Carrot Juice?

DAVID. We're all out of Carrot Juice.

RABBIT. I'm dead on.

MARK. Are you?

RABBIT. Yeah.

MARK *takes his cigarettes out and offers one towards*
DAVID. *DAVID takes one.* MARK *takes one and then puts*
the cigarettes away. RABBIT *watches them.*

MARK. Oh, where's my manners?

MARK *takes the cigarettes out, pretending that he forgot*
about RABBIT *and offers them to* RABBIT. *RABBIT*
shakes his head.

RABBIT. Don't smoke.

MARK. Smart. These things'll kill you. But then so will
joining the UDA.

RABBIT. That's why I didn't join.

DAVID. Driving cars over a hundred miles an hour in estates
that weren't really built for it will kill you too.

MARK. And quicker.

RABBIT. I'd rather die at a hundred miles an hour behind the
wheel of a sports car than slumped over my desk with a
heart attack.

MARK (*coughs*). Is that directed at me? (*Clutches chest,*
coughs more.)

RABBIT. Or down the alley, (*Performs the action.*) bullet in
the back of the head.

DAVID (*laughs*). Is that a threat? (*Fakes heart scare brought*
on by fear.)

RABBIT. Just saying.

MARK. You could have a heart attack you know.

RABBIT. Not me.

MARK. Oh you could. It's not just these things that go for
your heart. Fear can go for it too.

RABBIT *points at his knuckles. 'NO FEAR' is written*
across both hands.

MARK. Nof ear. Is there something wrong with your ear?

RABBIT. No Fear. You have to read right across.

MARK. Looks like nof ear to me.

RABBIT. That's one word, right across.

MARK. You really thought that out very well didn't you, Rabbit.

RABBIT. No Fear.

RABBIT *realises his own accidental joke.*

MARK. Are you saying that you're not afraid of anything?

DAVID. You'd be a brave man to join the UDA like in these troubled times.

RABBIT *glares at* DAVID.

MARK. My girlfriend is afraid of spiders. It's a phobia really more than a fear.

DAVID. I don't like aeroplanes.

MARK. That's a phobia too isn't it?

DAVID. I don't think so. I think a phobia would be more if it was an unrealistic fear. Like a spider isn't really going to kill you but if an aeroplane crashes . . .

MARK. Still improbable though. They say it's safer than crossing the roads.

DAVID. Especially if Rabbit here happens to be out on one of his wee joyriding expeditions.

MARK. The fear of prison would be a phobia.

DAVID (*quietly*). Yes it would.

MARK. Providing it was just a fear of the building but if you were like afraid of being locked in a room with five big Catholic men who might just be missing their girlfriends. That would be like a real fear.

DAVID. I think I'd rather take my chances on the road.

MARK. You could make it improbable or in fact impossible though.

DAVID. How?

MARK. Well if you admitted to being in the UDA for instance then they would put you in a UDA wing and Catholics wouldn't be able to get near you.

DAVID. Unless your name was Billy Wright.

MARK. Wasn't in the UDA you see.

DAVID. True.

MARK (*to* RABBIT). What other benefits do the UDA offer these days?

RABBIT. I wouldn't know.

MARK. Were you not listening there?

RABBIT. I heard you.

MARK. Let me get to the point here. You have three options. Keep going the way you're going and you'll leave us no choice but to put you away for a very long time.

DAVID. A very long bad time in a real prison.

MARK. We're not talking Young Offenders Centre here.

RABBIT. I can handle myself.

DAVID. You might have to.

MARK. Option Two. You could admit to being a member of the UDA. We'll do everything we can to paint a picture of you as the most dangerous UDA man alive and you'll go to your wee UDA wing for the rest of your life.

DAVID. That's not a great deal but then it's not the worst deal either.

RABBIT. I'm not in the UDA.

MARK. Option Three. We charge you for the Joyriding but we will both appeal to the Judge for leniency and appear as character witnesses and guarantee you get another chance. Two years probation and penalty points. Do you understand what I'm talking about here?

RABBIT. No.

MARK. You see this wouldn't go on record as a deal. You wouldn't be classed or identified as a snitch. There would be no case brought against Stanley Brown that had you connected to it in anyway. You would just be a free man. And all you have to do is give me two things.

RABBIT. What like?

MARK. Number One. You give me your word that you will never steal another car. Never Joyride, never drive fast. Never drive recklessly.

RABBIT. What's Number Two, slit my own wrists?

DAVID. Good effort.

MARK. No, nothing as dramatic as that. Just give me a little bit of rope to hang Stanley out to dry. How does that sound?

RABBIT. Like mad dog shite.

MARK. That's not the attitude, Rabbit.

RABBIT. I stole the car, evaded your boys and crashed. No-one got hurt but me. I'll take my chances with the Judge. Maybe get a holiday out of it.

MARK. No. Not this time Kiddo.

MARK *takes the file from the bin and places it back on the table.* DAVID *paces.* MARK *and* DAVID *move to the door and whisper to one another. Occasionally they glance at* RABBIT. RABBIT *watches them.*

MARK. Tell me who picked the car, Rabbit?

RABBIT. What car?

MARK. The car you stole.

RABBIT. I picked it.

MARK. Who for but?

RABBIT. For myself.

MARK. No you didn't.

RABBIT. I fucking did.

DAVID. February 3rd, 1996 – Rabbit stole his first car.

MARK. Where?

DAVID. In town.

MARK. Where did he take it?

DAVID. Nowhere he just drove round and round and round until he crashed.

MARK. So he wasn't actually going anywhere.

DAVID. No.

MARK. How many people were in the car?

DAVID. Including himself, four.

MARK. A girl?

DAVID. Yes.

MARK. Showing off.

DAVID. August 18th, 1996 – Rabbit's at it again.

MARK. Where did he steal this car?

DAVID. In town.

MARK. Where did he take it?

DAVID. Nowhere, he just drove round and round until he crashed it.

MARK. Did he have any people in the car?

DAVID. Three others.

MARK. Same people.

DAVID *pretends to check the pages in front of him.*

DAVID. Two of them the same.

MARK. Girl?

DAVID. Different girl.

MARK. That's interesting.

DAVID. March 17th, 1997.

MARK. St Patrick's Day.

DAVID. Stole a blue Ford.

MARK. Where?

DAVID. In town.

MARK. Town would've been bunged, did he take it away from all that?

DAVID. No.

MARK. He drove through the parades?

DAVID. No, he just drove round and round until he crashed it.

MARK. Really? How many people were stupid enough to go
with him this time?

DAVID. Three.

MARK. Any from the past?

DAVID. A couple.

MARK. Girl?

DAVID. Different girl.

MARK. I see a pattern building here. Do you Rabbit?

RABBIT. I don't know what the fuck you're on about.

MARK. Pick one at random.

DAVID *pretends to pick one at random.*

DAVID. January 3rd, 1998 – will that do?

MARK. Where did he steal it?

DAVID. Town.

MARK. Where did he take it?

DAVID. Nowhere.

MARK. He just drove it round and round . . .

DAVID. Until he crashed it.

MARK. Three other people in it?

DAVID. Exactly.

MARK. Different girl?

DAVID. I'd have to check.

DAVID *pretends to check.*

MARK. I don't have to check. It was a different girl wasn't it,
Rabbit. You're always faithful to your routine but not to the
girls.

DAVID. Different girl.

MARK. Told you.

DAVID. It's like a ritual. Is this what you do when you change
girlfriend?

MARK. Read the last one.

DAVID. The BM?

MARK. Where did he steal it?

DAVID. Glengormley.

MARK. Not in town?

DAVID. It says Glengormley here.

MARK. But he took it in to town, did he?

DAVID. No he took it into Rathcoole.

MARK. Really? Was this to impress his new girlfriend?

DAVID. Not unless he was picking her up somewhere.

MARK. How do you mean?

DAVID. Well, when he crashed this time he was on his own.

MARK. On his own. That can't be right. Can we get someone to check this out?

RABBIT. I was on my own, so what, that doesn't prove anything.

MARK. No? You don't think so.

DAVID. I think it's fairly clear.

MARK. Let me tell you what it proves, son. It's not the same. The same thing wasn't happening here. This wasn't a Joyride this was something else.

RABBIT. No it wasn't.

DAVID. The Judge won't like that.

MARK. The Judge doesn't need to know about it.

DAVID. Oh he does, I have to tell him.

MARK. No, I want to drop it. I want to lose the evidence. I want to make a mistake so as this all goes away and little Bunny here goes free.

RABBIT. I stole a car in New Mossley one time. I was by myself and I brought it to Rathcoole just to drive it round and round until it couldn't go anymore.

MARK. Check the file.

DAVID *pretends to check the file.*

MARK. When was this?

RABBIT. Last Sep . . . Not last year but the year before.

MARK. Any luck?

DAVID. What kind of car was it?

RABBIT. It was a Rover. One year old.

MARK. Let me see.

   DAVID *passes the file to* MARK.

DAVID. I can't find it.

RABBIT. It has to be in there.

MARK. Can't find it.

DAVID. Do you want me to check with the TACT boys?

MARK. No.

RABBIT. They'll tell you. When it crashed I burnt it on the
   football pitches.

MARK. Sorry. It's not here.

DAVID. You don't think someone's misplaced that one do
   you?

MARK. How?

DAVID. These UDA guys have friends everywhere.

RABBIT. I'm not in the UDA.

MARK. Your luck's dead, kiddo. It's not in here so I'm afraid
   we can't use it to help you out. See that's the thing about
   evidence. We gather evidence and we may or may not use it
   against you.

RABBIT. Use it to fucking suit yourselves you mean.

MARK. He's learning.

DAVID. He's quick.

Interview Room A

BILL *stubs his cigarette out and moves to the tape recorder.* BILL *takes the tapes out and seals them. Once sealed they must be signed.* BILL *signs his part and passes them to* STANLEY *for signature.* STANLEY *signs the tapes.*

STANLEY. I want name and address. Phone number if possible. Car – Make, model, colour and registration.

BILL. Who for?

STANLEY. Her.

BILL. What?

STANLEY. Just get it.

ACT TWO

Interview Room A

CAROLINE *is sitting reading through files.* MARK *enters carrying a package from the Chinese Takeaway. He takes one little bag, obviously from an expensive Chinese Restaurant, containing* CAROLINE*'s lunch and places the other, his lunch, on the table.*

MARK. Do you realise Judy almost caught me coming in here with this?

CAROLINE. Better you than me.

MARK. Thanks very much.

CAROLINE. I mean better you than me because of your charm.

MARK. It's not charm that works with Judy, it's people skills.

CAROLINE. People skills?

MARK. That's what David calls it.

CAROLINE. It's better than the canteen.

MARK. The food or the ambience?

CAROLINE. Don't forget the company.

MARK. Me or my files?

CAROLINE*'s phone rings.* CAROLINE *checks the caller's identity while* MARK *takes his coat off and hangs it on the back of a chair. As* CAROLINE *answers the phone she begins to open the separate containers.* MARK *snatches a couple of Prawn Crackers.* CAROLINE *raps his knuckles with a chopstick.*

CAROLINE. Hello honey. (*Listens.*) I know I said I would ring but I've literally stopped five seconds ago.

Mockingly, MARK *gestures to* CAROLINE *his disapproval of her lies.*

CAROLINE (*rolls her eyes and diverts her gaze, listens*).
Really? Was he delighted? (*Pause.*) Excellent. I'm sure he'll
be fine. (*Listens.*) That teacher Mr Lewis, he's going. You
liked him. Tall man, thin moustache. At the last parents-
teachers day you and him got on like a house on fire, do
you remember? (*Little listen.*) That's him. Yes, he's
definitely going. I don't know if he's in charge but he's
definitely going. That's one of the reasons I felt so OK
about it. (*Listens.*) He'll be fine. Did you get Maggie there
in time for the swimming? (*Little listen.*) Just checking.
(*Listens.*) I'm on my lunch now. It's just come through the
door I'd better eat it before it gets cold. (*Listens.*) It's not
going too well . . . it's all right . . . I might have to work late
though. (*Listens.*) I know, I know. I'll make it up to you.

When CAROLINE *hangs up she realises that* MARK *is
eating a Cheeseburger and Gravy Chip.*

CAROLINE (*horrified*). I don't understand you.

MARK. What?

MARK *munches into the Burger.*

CAROLINE. You go to a Chinese Restaurant and you get that.

MARK. I love this.

CAROLINE. It's Chippy food.

MARK. I got napkins.

MARK *wipes some sauce from his cheek.*

CAROLINE. You know what I mean.

MARK. Well I don't like all that other stuff.

CAROLINE. What have you tried?

MARK. All of it. Well . . .

CAROLINE. Name the ones you actually tried to eat.

MARK. I had some Chicken once. Didn't taste like Chicken.

CAROLINE. It's not supposed to.

MARK. Huh! Excuse me but when I order Chicken, tasting
like Chicken is a minimum requirement for me. Call me
peculiar.

CAROLINE. You must have got Chinese Style.

MARK. Well that's what I don't like about it.

CAROLINE. Why go to a Chinese Restaurant then?

MARK. They do great Burgers.

MARK *takes an extra large bite and* CAROLINE *shakes her head in disbelief.* CAROLINE *is quite adept with the Chopsticks.* DAVID *enters carrying a cup of tea.*

DAVID. I thought I'd find you here.

MARK. What is it?

DAVID *notices the chips.*

DAVID. Chips!

MARK *pushes the bag towards him.* DAVID *takes a couple, burning his fingers and his mouth.*

MARK. They're hot.

DAVID. How's it going Caroline?

CAROLINE. Usual. What about you?

DAVID. We'd a good morning. Hadn't we? (*Looks to* MARK *and continues.*) We were really rocking and rolling towards the end.

CAROLINE. Yeah?

DAVID. I'm learning a lot from this wily old fox.

MARK. Not so much of the 'old', thank you very much.

DAVID. Sorry Old School.

MARK *tries to ignore* DAVID.

CAROLINE. Did Mark give him the old one-two? Good Cop, Bad Cop. The entire repertoire of interrogation from A to B.

DAVID *laughs.*

DAVID. She's got your number.

MARK. Did you actually come in here for something?

CAROLINE. He smelt the chips.

DAVID *goes for more chips.* MARK *prevents him by shielding them with his arm.*

MARK. Answer the question first.

DAVID. I just came in to share some quality time with the Master.

MARK *allows him to have another chip.*

CAROLINE. You do realise he means me.

MARK (*sarcastically*). Yeah right.

DAVID. I was actually looking for Bill.

CAROLINE. Is he not in the office?

DAVID. No.

MARK. He's probably in the pub.

DAVID. Tried that too.

MARK. That's me all out.

CAROLINE. He'll be around. We're starting back soon.

DAVID. You're keen.

CAROLINE. We've one more hour after lunch and then I have to let him go.

DAVID. How's it looking?

CAROLINE. Do you want some of this? I've suddenly lost my appetite.

DAVID. That bad?

CAROLINE *moves her food towards* DAVID *and he begins to eat with the chopsticks.*

MARK. You have to just keep at him.

DAVID. He'll crack sooner or later.

CAROLINE. I don't have a later.

CAROLINE *begins to pace.*

DAVID. How's Bill been?

CAROLINE. Fucking useless.

DAVID. I'll tell him you said that.

MARK. You'll tell him nothing.

DAVID (*quickly*). I was joking.

CAROLINE. I better go and track him down.

DAVID. I'll go. I have to anyway.

CAROLINE. Who was looking for him?

DAVID. Solicitor I think.

CAROLINE. You think.

DAVID. I was just coming back from lunch and I was told to get him.

MARK. Go get him then.

CAROLINE. Who actually told you to get him?

DAVID. The Inspector.

CAROLINE *thinks about this.* MARK *nods* DAVID *towards the door and* DAVID *leaves.*

MARK. What's going on?

CAROLINE. Bill's fucking me about.

MARK. Is this your paranoia kicking in again?

CAROLINE. I wish it was.

MARK. The Inspector doing this report is really going for your nerves.

CAROLINE. They're having meetings behind my back. Talking about me.

MARK. It's probably unrelated.

CAROLINE. That would be some coincidence.

MARK. Bill's not exactly the perfect cop. Seems to me that the Inspector would be calling him in to tick him off privately on a regular basis. Who knows what it might be this time?

CAROLINE. I don't think so.

MARK. It's more likely that he's keeping an eye on Bill. It happens. I was five years in before I worked with a female detective. It's boy's own club and all that. (MARK *watches* CAROLINE *frown.*) Don't let it get you down. The Inspector knows he has to work against all that nowadays.

CAROLINE. What are you trying to say? That he'll give me a good report just because I'm a woman.

MARK. Give me some credit. What I'm saying is that he'll give you a report based on your ability. If there is an important factor that swings it then it'll be your most recent cases. It always goes like that because that's what's going to be fresh in his mind.

CAROLINE. Well that's my problem. My most recent cases have been disasters. Mostly caused by Bill.

MARK. He'll know that. I mean you don't see him recommending Bill for promotion, do you?

CAROLINE. True.

MARK. I worked with a Catholic Detective once. This guy thought everybody was watching him, everybody was out to get him.

CAROLINE. But surely he must've been right.

MARK. No, what I'm saying is he thought it was everybody and all the time. Not just when promotion boards came round.

CAROLINE. How long ago was this?

MARK. That's not the point.

CAROLINE. If you're going to sit there and tell me that nobody was really out to get this Catholic guy then . . . (*Almost laughs.*)

MARK. Caroline, lots of people were out to get him, of course they were, it was a different world back then.

CAROLINE. Oh of course I forgot we've got peace now, we've got progress. Mark, if that's what you want to believe then go ahead and believe it but don't talk to me because I live in the real world.

MARK. I live in the real world too Caroline.

CAROLINE. What about you and this Catholic guy, how did that go?

MARK. I liked him. I thought we worked well together. Once I learned how to deal with his little outbursts, you know.

CAROLINE. Is that what you're doing with me?

MARK (*laughs lightly*). No.

Pause.

CAROLINE. Do you see him much now?

MARK. Last time I saw him was shortly after the IRA tried to kill him. And you think you have problems?

CAROLINE. I know there are people worse off but that doesn't make it any easier.

MARK. Well if it helps, he got promoted while he was working with me.

CAROLINE. Are you making this up?

MARK. Check the files.

CAROLINE. That's maybe going to be the difference. The Catholic guy got you and I got Bill.

MARK. If that's the way it goes then you need to talk to the Inspector about that. Maybe move on.

CAROLINE. Trying to get rid of me now are you?

MARK. No.

Pause.

CAROLINE. I've a confession to make by the way.

MARK (*jokingly*). Should I start the tape?

CAROLINE. I got Bill to go out and ask Judy for tea.

MARK. That's a waste of time.

CAROLINE. Not really, I knew there would be a rigmarole and that would buy me some time.

MARK. Was he raging?

CAROLINE. While he was away I had a go at Stanley Brown about the UDA using joyriders.

MARK. Off the record? (*Watches* CAROLINE *nod.*) How did he react?

CAROLINE. I thought I saw something in his eyes. (*Pause.*) Maybe it's something you could use with Rabbit.

MARK. I've got Rabbit by the balls. I just need to figure out how I can get him to give us something to help you sooner rather than later.

CAROLINE. You've got to get me something within the next forty-five minutes. Fifty minutes top.

BILL *enters the room.*

MARK. Bill!

CAROLINE. Where were you?

BILL. Lunch.

CAROLINE. Where'd you go?

BILL. Pub.

CAROLINE. A new pub?

MARK *realises* BILL *is becoming annoyed.*

MARK. Someone was looking for you.

CAROLINE. The Inspector.

BILL. I saw him.

CAROLINE *watches* BILL. MARK *stands and begins to clear the table into a bucket. The three exchange looks.*

CAROLINE. I'll go and get Muteman.

BILL (*immediately*). I'll go and get him.

MARK *clears the table and walks to the door with the bucket.*

CAROLINE. Check the tape and I'll be back in a minute.

BILL. Why are we starting back so soon?

CAROLINE. Do I really have to answer that question?

BILL. No.

CAROLINE *and* MARK *leave* BILL *looking very nervous.*

BILL. Shit! Shit! Shit!

BILL *paces, thinking and worrying. Eventually* BILL *sets up the tape recorder and waits.* CAROLINE *leads* STANLEY *back into the interview room.* STANLEY *sits.* BILL *takes his normal seat.*

CAROLINE (*sighs*). Here we go again. Interview recommences at 12.52.

BILL. Do you want me to start?

CAROLINE *looks a little surprised.*

CAROLINE. Go ahead, Sherlock.

BILL *stands and paces.* CAROLINE *waits.* STANLEY *looks puzzled.*

BILL. Stop the tape.

CAROLINE *is intrigued.* BILL *walks out into the corridor.*

CAROLINE. Interview suspended 12.53.

CAROLINE *looks to* BILL. *Eventually* CAROLINE *follows him.*

Corridor

BILL. Could you leave us alone for a minute?

CAROLINE. No. I'd rather not.

BILL. I want a moment.

CAROLINE. Sorry. I'm too intrigued. But feel free to take this anywhere you want.

BILL. I'm asking you for a few minutes to talk to Stanley.

CAROLINE. You had that earlier Bill.

BILL *stands frustrated.*

BILL. Do you want to go with me and we'll see the Inspector?

CAROLINE. We don't have time Bill. Just pretend I'm not there.

BILL *walks away.* CAROLINE *follows.*

BILL. You said I had to learn to improvise. That's what I'm trying to do.

CAROLINE. Well I need to watch you so as I can tell you how you're doing.

BILL. I need a moment alone. He thinks I'm the Good Cop. I want five minutes to see if I can use that to sort this out.

CAROLINE. I can give you ten minutes.

BILL. Thank you.

CAROLINE. But not alone.

BILL. Caroline?

CAROLINE *returns to the Interview Room.* BILL *follows her.*

Interview Room A

CAROLINE (*to* STANLEY). I'm sorry, are we keeping you from something?

BILL *returns a look that suggests she should play along.*

BILL. I'm thinking on my feet here, Stanley. I need you to help me out.

STANLEY *looks to* CAROLINE *and then back to* BILL.

BILL. Organisations change. Look at mine. If someone had told me when I was doing my training that thirty years later I would be standing in a room taking orders from a young girl I would've . . . I don't know what I would've done.

CAROLINE. Run to the hills.

BILL *looks at* STANLEY *as though to say 'see what I mean?'*

BILL. I didn't run to the hills. I stood my ground. I adapted. I changed.

CAROLINE *signals to* BILL *that time is running out and that he should speed things up.*

BILL. You're probably saying to yourself, 'Where's he going with this?' Well Stanley, let me tell you something, off the record. The tapes stopped. We have a flimsy case against you that we're not prepared to take on but what you don't know is that we have other people in other rooms talking their arses off. Now you have to think about this. If one of them, any one of them, gives us something that we can run with, we will be forced to run with it and prosecute you. (*Pause.*) But I personally don't want to waste my time doing that. Let's face it, we know that you're in the UDA but you're not exactly running the show are you? No, you're not. You are in a similar position to me. It might not seem that way right now but think about it. Your organisation is changing too and there's nothing you can do to stop it, or is there? See I know like you know that there are other more important people out there, causing all these changes. Changes that affect you and me both. Changes that affect our culture, our identity, our country. You know the people I'm talking about. The UDA Inner Circle for a start. I'm just trying to be honest with you. I'd much rather have them in here than you.

STANLEY *says nothing.* CAROLINE *paces, becoming more interested in* BILL*'s line.*

BILL. Can I ask you something, Stanley? Are you happy with the way this great peace process is going?

CAROLINE *for a moment thinks* STANLEY *is going to respond.*

BILL. I don't think you are. I'm not. Do you want me to tell you why?

STANLEY *glares at* BILL *suspiciously.*

BILL. I don't think it is a peace process for a start. I think it is a Nationalist process. I think it's playing into the hands of the enemies of Ulster. I don't believe David Trimble when he says that the Union is safer now than it ever was. I don't believe the Irish Government when they lifted their territorial claim over Northern Ireland. But I do believe Gerry Adams when he says that this is a stepping stone to a United Ireland. I can see it in his eyes and he believes it and I believe it. Do you?

Silence.

BILL *seems to be talking to* CAROLINE *more than* STANLEY.

BILL. Now the reason I'm telling you all this will become clear. I've been in the RUC for over thirty years. Way before you were born. As far as I was concerned I joined a Protestant Police force to protect the Protestant people of Ulster against the IRA. People only began to think of them as a serious threat back then and that was my main reason for joining. The UVF was underground and illegal already, so being a law-abiding Protestant I didn't see any future in that. But in the early seventies when the Vanguard produced the UDA I saw possibilities there. We all did. It was almost like a reserve police force, isn't that right?

STANLEY *nods.* CAROLINE *takes her seat, her eyes betraying her enthusiasm.*

BILL. Together we defended Ulster for the next twenty years and then when the British Government decided to betray us and banned the UDA we had to change. We in the RUC were no longer permitted to have any association with UDA members and since then as I'm sure you've noticed things have got worse and worse.

STANLEY *nods again and flicks his eyes towards* CAROLINE. CAROLINE *studies him.*

BILL. The Nationalists are after us now. After a very successful campaign against you guys they've now decided to try and get rid of us. Take a look around, 'The Patten Report', what a joke that is. Take the guns off the Police but let the terrorists keep theirs for 'personal protection'. 'Disband the RUC now'. I must pass a hundred of those signs everyday on my way home. It kills me. 'Over my dead body' that's what I say. And this is the point. This is why I want to talk to you in here, right now. (*Pause.*) If we're to stop this current trend of conceding to every Nationalist whim then we have to work together. It doesn't have to be me and you. And of course it can't be out in the open it has to be behind closed doors. But in order for us to start that process we have to get rid of the people who are in the way. And that's the people at the top of your organisation.

BILL *paces.* CAROLINE *waits, watching* BILL *and then returning to* STANLEY.

BILL. I've sat in this station and watched my own organisation crumble. We even have Catholics involved these days. And the government wants more and more of them brought in. If they had their way the IRA would take over the Police force. Seriously, education today, security tomorrow. Promotion and recruitment is going to be at least fifty-fifty. Is our population even fifty-fifty? No. That's reverse discrimination, Stanley and we're going to suffer, in years to come you're going to be in here being interviewed by two Catholics, do you hear me? Men like me are going to be ignored for promotion after promotion and then eventually shelved. In situations like Drumcree or other civil disturbances, who is going to be enforcing the law, who is going to be making the decisions? In short who is going to be protecting your community? No-one. Every decision about a march. Every decision about anything is going to go their way. Everything in fact is going to go their way. We can't let that happen. So that's why I'm saying to you that I've also sat here and watched your organisation crumble. Yeah. Are you going to tell me that you haven't thought these things yourself? Money, that's all they seem to be interested in, admittedly I'm talking as an outsider, but that's how I see it. Am I wrong? Some say the good ones pack it in and involve themselves in politics. Like there's no money in that, know what I'm saying? (*Pause*.) If you give us something, we'll put them away and who will take their place? People like you Stanley. People like you, who care about Ulster. People like you, who know that in order to protect the Protestant people you need our help. So, we need yours.

STANLEY *doesn't respond.* CAROLINE *is more frustrated than* BILL.

CAROLINE. Come on, Stanley. Talk to Bill, he's your friend.

BILL *walks away.* CAROLINE *moves in.*

CAROLINE. Let me tell you this. If you don't start talking. And we put the tape back on and finish the interview with nothing. You will go free but this offer will never be on the table again.

BILL. What do you say Stanley?

CAROLINE. For God and Ulster?

BILL. Give us anything on anybody.

CAROLINE. As long as we can use it, we'll go with it.

BILL. Do you not trust us? Well, here's why you should, think about this, we will be able to use this case in our favour. By arresting a senior member of the UDA it will not only clear the way for you and then our relationship with you but it will also give us a nice bit of publicity to use against all those people and organisations who are after us. It's beautiful.

CAROLINE *and* BILL *wait.* STANLEY *looks away.*

CAROLINE. This is your last chance. And before you give us your final answer think about this. Once you take yourself out of the picture we will be forced to go after someone else and if we get someone else and they move up, where will that leave you? Because you're the first threat and we will give them your name and they will realise that you'll have to go too. And when I say go, I mean go.

BILL. Caroline, give me one minute alone.

CAROLINE. It's not working Bill.

BILL. It might if you left the room.

CAROLINE. Is this a man thing? Is it Stanley?

BILL *walks away.*

CAROLINE. Is my presence in this room offending you?

BILL. Don't listen to her, Stanley. Listen to me. If you want us to talk privately you've only to request it. Or if you want a solicitor I can go and organise that and maybe talk to him.

Telephone rings. CAROLINE *is raging with herself and steps away to check the name of the caller.*

CAROLINE (*quietly as she goes*). Sorry.

BILL *glares at* STANLEY *and moves as close to him as possible when* CAROLINE *has moved away.* CAROLINE *realises that her phone isn't ringing and turns back.* CAROLINE *looks at* BILL *who has to step away from* STANLEY.

CAROLINE. Stand up. Raise your hands.

STANLEY *stands and raises his arms in the air.* CAROLINE *begins to search* STANLEY *and discovers a mobile phone.* CAROLINE *steps away leaving* STANLEY *holding his arms high.*

CAROLINE. How the fuck did you get this in?

BILL. Let me see it.

CAROLINE *walks away.*

CAROLINE. Will we answer it?

Telephone stops ringing. CAROLINE *waits.*

BILL. I wouldn't advise that. Let me see it.

CAROLINE. Wait, they might be stupid enough to leave a message. (*To* STANLEY.) I take it this isn't your personal telephone with all your numbers logged and ready for me. I mean I just know I'm not that lucky.

STANLEY. I found that in the corridor.

CAROLINE (*as though shocked to hear the voice*). Who the fuck said that? Did you throw your voice there Bill? You're very good.

BILL. Where did you find it?

STANLEY. I told you, I found it in the corridor.

BILL. Why didn't you hand it in immediately?

CAROLINE. Why didn't you hand it to the Officer who was with you?

STANLEY *looks to* BILL. CAROLINE *sees this.* BILL *looks away.*

BILL. I'll take it down to the desk and see who's lost it.

CAROLINE. Have you used this since it was in your possession?

STANLEY *looks away.*

CAROLINE. Start the tape again Bill.

BILL. I don't think that's really necessary.

CAROLINE. Oh no. Let me be the judge of that.

BILL. There's nowhere to go with it. He found it, he didn't make any calls and now we've got it back. Let me take it down and see who's lost it. You never know they might be waiting on that call. And it might be private so let me have it.

BILL *reaches out towards the telephone.* CAROLINE *presses the buttons and listens to the message.* BILL *and* STANLEY *exchange worried looks.* CAROLINE *looks at* STANLEY *and then* BILL. BILL *waits becoming more and more nervous.* CAROLINE *hangs up the phone.*

CAROLINE. It's logged.

BILL. What did it say?

CAROLINE. It said you've to phone your wife, Bill.

CAROLINE *walks out of the room.*

BILL. Fuck me.

STANLEY. Relax.

BILL. You really are out of your fucking mind.

STANLEY. It could've been worse, it could've been the boys.

BILL. I'm fucked here.

BILL *walks towards the door.*

STANLEY. Bill?

BILL *stops and turns towards* STANLEY.

STANLEY. I really liked where you were going with your wee speech there. Maybe we could talk about it for real some time soon. Just sit down. She's running low on time Bill.

BILL. That bitch! That fucking bitch!

They wait.

Corridor

CAROLINE *walks towards Interview Room B followed by* MARK *and* DAVID.

MARK. What are you?

CAROLINE. Get him out of there.

MARK. David?

DAVID (*opens door Interview Room A*). Detective Byrne?

BILL *follows him out.*

Interview Room B

MARK. Do you want to tell me what's going on?

CAROLINE. He'll tell you himself.

DAVID *and* BILL *enter Interview Room B.*

CAROLINE. This is the end of the line for you, Bill.

MARK. Relax, Caroline.

CAROLINE. Don't tell me to relax. I've spent over sixty hours trying to break this bastard and all that time he's something going on with him behind my back.

BILL. You can't prove a thing.

CAROLINE. He had your phone.

BILL. So he stole my phone what does that prove?

MARK. So you're saying he stole your phone?

BILL. You know what these guys are like. Nimble fingers.
They could steal the eyes out of your head.

CAROLINE. He knows it's worse than that or he wouldn't be
in here talking with us.

BILL. I'm just trying to save us all the embarrassment. You
know what she's like, Mark.

CAROLINE. I'm very tempted to just go to the Inspector.

BILL. You see.

MARK. Nobody's going to the Inspector.

BILL. You know it's nothing. Or you would have gone to him
right away.

CAROLINE. The only reason I haven't is because I'm not sure
how far up this goes.

MARK. Caroline, think about what you're saying.

CAROLINE. Talk to me.

DAVID. Are you saying that Bill leant him the phone? Why?
Why would he do that?

BILL. Exactly right. And even if I did what would that prove?

MARK. So are you saying you did lend him it Bill?

BILL. No, I'm saying he stole it. And that's it. But I'd prefer to
keep it between us.

CAROLINE. I wonder why.

DAVID. Because taking it any further would mean admitting
he stole the phone right here under our noses.

BILL. That's what I want to avoid.

MARK. The only thing you could consider doing is using it
against him.

CAROLINE. How?

MARK. Tell him you're prepared to do him for theft of property.

BILL. We probably couldn't even prove that.

MARK. You don't have to prove it Bill, just use it as leverage to make him panic.

CAROLINE. There's no way he stole this from you. You gave him it.

BILL. I did not.

CAROLINE. Just tell me why.

MARK. Is there something going on with you Bill?

BILL. There's nothing going on.

CAROLINE. There is.

DAVID. What like?

MARK. Bill, I'm going to give you one chance mate. If you tell me now that you want to talk about something I'll agree to it. If you tell me it has to be private . . .

CAROLINE. No way.

DAVID. Leave it Caroline.

MARK. It's all up to you Bill but the thing is that this is the only time I'm prepared to listen to you. If you make me jump through hoops I'm not going to be happy and I'm not going to give you another chance later on.

BILL *thinks about his options very carefully.*

CAROLINE. You better start talking or I'm walking. And I'll take this a lot higher than the Inspector.

DAVID. Pardon my saying so Caroline but I think this is something you need to sort out in private. I mean think about how the Inspector would view this. And how he would write it in your report.

CAROLINE *walks away despairingly.*

MARK. What's it going to be Bill?

BILL. I'm happy enough to sort it out here between us.

MARK. Caroline?

They wait for CAROLINE. CAROLINE *turns back towards them.*

CAROLINE. I'll sort it out in here if you talk to me.

DAVID. What are you getting at, Caroline?

CAROLINE. Collusion.

BILL. Bullshit.

DAVID. That's a very serious accusation.

Pause.

MARK. Why don't you take a break Caroline and let us talk to Bill.

CAROLINE. No way.

DAVID. Does that sound all right to you Bill?

BILL *nods.*

MARK. Get some tea, coffee, go to the loo whatever, just give us ten minutes.

CAROLINE *glares with real hatred at* BILL. MARK *and* DAVID *wait.*

MARK. Unless you don't trust me.

CAROLINE *looks in* MARK*'s eyes.*

CAROLINE. I'll give you ten minutes.

MARK. You're doing the right thing.

CAROLINE. Well you're the only one I do trust so . . . don't let me down.

DAVID. Thanks very much Caroline.

CAROLINE *looks at* DAVID *almost apologetically then returns to* MARK. MARK*'s eyes haven't left her.* CAROLINE *leaves.* BILL *sighs.* MARK *paces.*

DAVID. What's going on big man?

MARK. Are you going to talk to us properly Bill? You know me, you know you don't want to try to play me.

BILL. Don't be giving me the interrogation technique just hear me out.

MARK. Is this for the record?

MARK *moves towards the tape recorder.*

BILL. Touch the tape and my lips are sealed.

DAVID. What's going on here?

MARK. Let's find out . . . Bill?

MARK *and* DAVID *sit facing* BILL.

BILL. I'm going to take a chance with you Mark. I have to tell you something. I'm fucked here. I really am, you know.

DAVID. What?

MARK *indicates to* DAVID *that he should keep quiet for a while.* DAVID *can't believe what he is hearing.*

BILL. I've been on the force for over thirty years and I've seen a lot of shit and I've done some shit too. You know what I mean.

MARK. You have to get to the point Bill. She'll be back in ten minutes.

BILL. I've been up for promotion like her. I've been up three times. Glowing recommendations. (*Stops.*) There was this one time when I was so sure that it was my turn.

DAVID. You can never be sure about a thing like that.

MARK. Keep talking.

BILL. I took loans. I, you know, I got in over my head and when it all fell apart I tried to pay them off but what little money I had I invested badly. I took a bad hit, you know and then I borrowed again to try and pay off the first loan and then I got into a cycle. It could've happened to anybody. It was the worst run of bad luck you could ever imagine.

MARK. They bought your debt?

DAVID. Who?

MARK. The UDA.

DAVID. No. No way.

BILL *nods.*

MARK. What way have you been paying it off since?

BILL. Little things.

MARK. Like lending people your phone.

BILL. You have to understand I was about to lose my house, my car, my wife. Everything. I'm telling you, I know what you're thinking. You're thinking what a bastard and I would've thought the same of you if you were standing here telling me this. I know other guys and I've looked at them and I've thought exactly the same thing.

MARK. How bad is this Bill?

BILL. At first it was just little things, Mark. Little bits of information. Mostly harmless stuff but then when they wanted more I had nothing but they wouldn't accept that so they came after me.

DAVID. Who?

BILL. The big guns. Fuck me David they've even threatened my family.

MARK. And you rolled over for them.

BILL. What else could I do?

MARK. You could've fought them.

BILL. You can't fight these people.

DAVID. You could've come to us. We could've helped you. We could've used it.

BILL. I didn't know what to do. Honestly, I was frightened. I was a mess. The only thing I could do, I know this sounds terrible but it's true, the only thing I could do was watch everything fall apart and that's exactly what I've been doing. Besides I'm coming to you now.

MARK. You've been caught Bill.

DAVID. This can't leave this room.

MARK. I'll be the judge of that.

DAVID. I'm serious. Look at the papers, look at the TV, they're all over us. This would be another nail in our coffin. This has to stay between us.

MARK. David, sit down.

BILL. I would obviously prefer it if it stayed in here too.

MARK. Here's the deal Bill, if you tell me everything then there's a chance it might stay between us but if I feel for some reason that you're not being one hundred per cent honest with me . . .

DAVID. Then what?

MARK. Then we take him down.

BILL. Then I'll deny it again.

MARK. I'm sure there are other holes in this Bill. Do you really want to go down that road with me?

BILL. No, not at all.

MARK. Why did he want your phone?

BILL. I want a deal.

DAVID. What is it Bill? What have you done?

BILL. It's Caroline.

> MARK *suppresses his anger momentarily.*

DAVID. What about her?

BILL. That's what he wanted the phone for.

> MARK *tries to get over the desk.* BILL *jumps to his feet and moves backwards away from it.* DAVID *grabs at* MARK *to prevent him.* MARK *has the hold of* BILL.

DAVID. Let go of him. Let go of him Mark for fuck sake.

> MARK *holds him for another few seconds.*

BILL. I'm trying to help you. I never wanted this.

MARK. What did you give them?

BILL. Her address and vehicle details.

DAVID. Let go of him Mark.

BILL. They already have mine Mark. It was me or her.

MARK. And you picked her you spineless bastard.

BILL. What else could I do?

DAVID. Let go of him now.

> MARK *lets go.* BILL *moves further away.* DAVID *positions himself between them.*

MARK. You're finished.

DAVID. We can use this.

BILL. I'll do anything.

MARK. We already know that.

DAVID. Can't we do Brown for this?

MARK. No we can't. Unless something happens. And you better start praying that that something doesn't happen.

DAVID. Then we let the bastard go and we'll wait for them to make contact, come on Mark, they're going to try and use Caroline like they've been using Bill.

MARK. Caroline would never agree to letting him go.

DAVID. She might have to if they have nothing to charge him with.

MARK. She's got this and she'll want something done. Besides we can't be sure that they want to use Caroline.

DAVID. Of course they do.

MARK. You don't know that David. This could be an attack, you know, a warning.

BILL. I think they only want to scare her and then maybe use her.

MARK. Shut the fuck up.

DAVID. They're Protestants for God's sake, they're not going to attack us.

MARK. We've relied on that logic for too long, David.

DAVID (*outraged*). For fuck sake. Let's go talk to Brown. You and me can sort this whole fucking thing out right now.

MARK. Here's what we're going to do. Send a car to pick up Caroline's husband, take him to the school to get the kids and take them all to a safe house. (*Pause.*) Take Bill down to the office and keep him away from Stanley Brown. And pick up everyone Brown called this morning.

DAVID. Fair enough.

MARK. And get Caroline back in here.

DAVID. Let's go Bill. Caroline?

DAVID *opens the door and* CAROLINE *comes back into the room.*

CAROLINE. Where's he going?

MARK. Come in and sit down.

CAROLINE *does so.* DAVID *takes* BILL *out.*

CAROLINE. Where's he going?

MARK. A safe distance from Stanley Brown.

CAROLINE. What's happening?

MARK. They've got your address and vehicle details.

CAROLINE. What?

MARK. We've sent a car to take Harry and the kids to a safe house.

CAROLINE. Bastards!

MARK. Caroline you need to consider your options.

CAROLINE. My options are very clear. I'm going to do Stanley Brown and then I'm going after Bill.

MARK. I'm not talking about those options. I'm talking about upgrading your security arrangements at home.

CAROLINE. Grills around the windows, access codes on the doors, two huge angry dogs in each garden and a giant neon sign on the roof, 'Cop lives here'. No thanks.

MARK. You could move.

CAROLINE. Not an option. I'm not going on the run. I'm not the criminal.

MARK. OK then, you could let Stanley go.

CAROLINE. I'd feel a little bit safer keeping him here.

MARK. You could let me do him and maybe he'll forget about you.

CAROLINE. He won't forget about me. He's made me a target, a big fuck-off flashing target and I'm going to make that the biggest mistake of his life. There's still a little time left.

MARK. Why don't you go to the safe house, see the kids and talk things over with Harry? You're exhausted. You're not getting anywhere.

CAROLINE. I must be getting somewhere if he's decided to have a go at me and my family.

DAVID *returns.*

DAVID. We've sent cars and organised a safe house near the beach.

MARK. The kids'll like that.

DAVID. Brown erased all calls he made but we're going to pick up McCready, Stevie Walsh and anyone else you can think of.

MARK. What about Hill's Cabs?

DAVID. Any known associates or usual suspects heading for Bangor will be scooped and brought here immediately.

CAROLINE. Thank you. That only leaves Bill.

MARK. Forget about Bill for the time being. You've got no case and if you take it to the Inspector you'll fuck up your promotion. You've seen the file David. Tell her?

DAVID. The complaints file?

MARK. Bill has maybe twenty separate complaints about you, Caroline.

CAROLINE. Petty things.

DAVID. Not when you add them up.

CAROLINE. It's a personality clash. Anyone can see that.

MARK. And when you go after Bill what way will they see that?

DAVID. You're not going after Bill.

CAROLINE. Am I not?

DAVID. We can't let her do that. (*To* CAROLINE.) Do you think Bill's the only person to file a complaint against you?

CAROLINE. You better be very careful what you say next.

DAVID. I'm not afraid of you.

MARK. David, we're trying to help here.

DAVID. We have our problems, sure we do just like any organisation, comes with the territory. But we don't need people pointing them out every five minutes. Or taking them outside.

CAROLINE. I've never taken anything outside.

DAVID. You don't think this would get out.

MARK. This isn't the point. The point here is you don't have enough to make a case against Bill.

DAVID. Wouldn't matter. Do you think the press wait around for evidence? Do you think they're going to examine the facts and make a fair assessment? Are they fuck? They would spread it all over the front pages. Within two days it would be World News. Maybe that's what you want. Mark, don't ask me to stand idly by and watch someone try to tear us apart.

CAROLINE. Someone like who?

MARK. Hey! We're not at war here.

DAVID. Are we not?

CAROLINE. Let me remind you who has seniority here.

DAVID. And she's up for promotion Mark.

MARK. What's that supposed to mean?

DAVID. It means in two weeks time she won't have to listen to you either. (*To* CAROLINE.) If you get this promotion and you keep on going what's the point if you suddenly turn round one day and there is no Police Force for you to be promoted to the top of? What are you going to do then?

CAROLINE. Will you talk to him and try to explain what this is about?

MARK. What is it about?

CAROLINE. What is it about? (*Pause.*) This is about me standing next door trying to build a case against a man who extorts money from businessmen, threatens old ladies who just happen to see him break the law and to top it all tries to threaten me and my family. Now are you going to stand idly by and let him get away with that?

DAVID. No I'm not.

MARK. He's not saying that.

CAROLINE. Or are you going to stand idly by while my supposed partner sets me up. Trades information with the very people we're investigating.

DAVID. I'm not saying that either.

CAROLINE. What are you saying then?

MARK. He's saying what I'm saying, you don't have a case.

CAROLINE. Then help me get one.

DAVID. We need to help Bill not go after him.

CAROLINE. Excuse me, but no.

DAVID. We're not internal affairs, Caroline. Mark?

MARK. It's all over for Bill.

DAVID. It doesn't have to be. He made a mistake, we all do.

CAROLINE. What mistakes have you made?

DAVID. The mistake I made was taking for granted the thirty odd years of service that Bill's so proud of and watching fast trackers like you treat him like shit.

MARK. That's enough David.

DAVID. Sorry.

CAROLINE. Thirty years of colluding with loyalists isn't that much to be proud of.

DAVID *is fuming but contains it very well.*

DAVID. Mark! Let's get Rabbit in here, break him and go after Brown. Let's concentrate on going after the real criminals.

MARK. That makes sense to me, Caroline what do you say?

CAROLINE. You don't get it do you? How many Bill's are there in this building?

DAVID. Here we go.

CAROLINE. I am not prepared to go on building cases against these scum bags only to turn round and see that in my own department some sympathetic loyalist has misplaced the evidence. Steered me the wrong way, blocked the investigation, traded information with the other side, gave up witnesses, sold me out, leant them a mobile phone and attacked my family.

DAVID. Then walk away. Because those are the pressures we all have to deal with on a daily basis.

CAROLINE. I say we have to deal with the criminals inside the force.

MARK. Caroline, I'm a bit confused. What are you asking me to do? Do you want me to take Bill down to the cells and kick the shit out of him to set an example for all the loyalist sympathisers on the force.

CAROLINE. Of course not.

MARK. 'Cause I will do it.

DAVID. This isn't about Loyalist sympathisers, there's as many IRA or Republican sympathisers on the force?

CAROLINE. No there's not.

DAVID. For fuck sake every time you turn round there's another Catholic promoted or another . . .

CAROLINE. Finish the sentence. (*Pause.*) Go ahead, finish it. You were going to say another woman, weren't you?

DAVID. Answer me this. Who controls the RUC, Caroline? Is it a Grand Master from the Orange Order? Is it the head of the UDA or the UVF? Is it anyone who considers themselves British or Loyal to the Royal Ulster Constabulary? I don't think so. I think if you really look at this corrupted and bigoted organisation as you and many like you are trying to make out you'll actually find that the people running the show are . . . big fat nothings. Neutrals, people who think they can sit on the fence and change sides at the drop of a hat. Well you can't. Like the Bible says, you're either for us or against us. And don't forget that these people turned us away from our traditional enemies to block, fight and hurt the people of our own communities.

MARK. Can we stop this please? This isn't going to help you, Caroline. We need to focus on what's immediately important. You've got your family safe for the time being. I would suggest that we have to concentrate our efforts on ensuring that safety becomes permanent or as near permanent as possible. Now, as far as the case goes, we've got next to nothing on anybody here and whilst I find that intolerable nonetheless it's the reality and we have to work on that basis. But I will personally guarantee to you now that I will do everything in my power and if David's willing you can assist me and we'll break Rabbit, give him a deal and he'll help us put Stanley Brown away for as long as we possibly can.

DAVID. What about Bill?

MARK. Bill's going to go home sick. He's been under a lot of pressure recently. He'll be on full pay for a year or so and then I'll recommend early retirement and we'll never have to worry about him again.

CAROLINE. Not good enough.

MARK. What you really have to think about Caroline is this. They got to Bill. He owed money, blah, blah, blah and they got him. Now they're going after you. And Northern Ireland is a very small place as we all know. You can only run or hide for so long before you find yourself back at square one. I mean you could just drop it, let Stanley go, walk away and save yourself and your family all this trouble. But, that's up to you and you alone.

CAROLINE. Is it? It doesn't feel like it.

MARK. If you got promoted they would move you away from here anyway. Maybe get you a desk job. And then go after the Bill's of this world.

DAVID. That's what you wanted all along isn't it?

CAROLINE. Yeah, I got up this morning and I said to myself 'I hope some scumbag terrorist threatens my family and my colleagues help him out'.

DAVID. I don't think you did. I think when you woke up this morning you wanted what every normal, decent human being wants. To feel safe. To leave their nice homes and go to their place of work with the knowledge that their home would be safe when they returned.

CAROLINE. Well that didn't happen.

DAVID. Why not?

CAROLINE. D'uh!

MARK. There's no time for this Caroline. You have to make a decision. What do you want to do?

CAROLINE. Go and get Rabbit.

MARK *leaves.*

DAVID. Let me tell you something policewoman of the year. You don't like me and that's fine I don't care too much for you either, it has to be said. But the reasons are different. Every time you fail and every time you let another Stanley Brown walk out of here you know that there are several men just outside the door who could've and would've done a better job and you feel ashamed because I think you are a very honest person and I think that you know in your heart that this is wrong. We can't go on promoting people to the top just because of their sex or their religion. It's wrong. Very wrong.

CAROLINE. Let me tell you what I know is very wrong, David. All these men that you're so proud of, every time they watch a Stanley Brown walking free from here they know in their hearts, if they're as honest as me, that they could've and should've helped me keep him here or at least not helped him go free. Maybe you think we should fast track those people to the top.

DAVID. People like me need to be at the top, Caroline and I'm not saying that from a macho point of view or a Protestant point of view. I'm saying I deserve to be at the top because I am the best man for the job. No-one knows more about our enemies than me. I put myself through university. I did every RUC training course going because I thought it was the smart thing to do if I wanted to get anywhere but to be honest Caroline I learned more about the Stanley Browns of this world just growing up in Rathcoole. I know them all, I know how they live, I know where they live. I know how they think, how they operate and I know how to keep them in line and break them when they step out of line. Besides me, what are the options, women running everything and for four days out of every month, we forget about judges and juries and just shoot anybody who looks like a criminal. We can't have that any more than we can have Catholics in charge of security I mean they think every Protestant in the world is guilty of everything from the famine to Bloody Sunday. Even the middle-class Catholics themselves want me here because they know I am that wall between them and the shit they came from. I am like the bridge they burnt. I am the steel ring around their house that keeps every scumbag, housebreaker, hijacker, joyrider, gluesniffer, dope-dealer, racketeer, petty criminal out of reach from their property, their house, their car, their belongings, their children, their neighbourhood. You are not. You know it. This whole thing proves it. You can't handle this, you can't handle Bill, you can't handle a case, a simple open and shut case, you let it slip through your hands. You're only here because you've got tits and you know it. Me, I'm here and I will always be here because tits don't get the job done, balls do.

MARK *returns with* RABBIT. DAVID *walks out of the room.*

CAROLINE. Follow me.

MARK. This interview is being tape recorded. The interview is being conducted in an interview room at Antrim Road Police Station. I am Detective Sergeant Simpson. The other Officer present is Detective Sergeant Patterson also attached to Antrim Road Police Station. The date is May 5th 2000 and the time is 1.37. Recommencing interview with Robert Montgomery. There is no other person present.

RABBIT. Is she your boss?

MARK. Partner.

RABBIT. Partner partner? I'd like a video of that.

CAROLINE. I've read your file, Robert. It is Robert isn't it?

MARK. Robert, Rabbit, he doesn't mind what you call him.

RABBIT. I've got thick skin, you can call me whatever you like as long as it's not too early in the morning.

MARK. He's got a thick head too.

RABBIT. Right down here.

RABBIT *grabs his own genitalia through his clothing and mocks* MARK.

RABBIT. Big thick head.

CAROLINE. I'm very happy for you but whilst that may be every little boys' dream it's not really going to help you out of this situation.

MARK. It's times like this that you need a quick head.

RABBIT. I can be quick.

MARK. I don't just mean behind the wheel of a car. Anybody can be quick behind the wheel of a car.

RABBIT. Not as quick as me they can't.

CAROLINE. Doesn't matter. On your feet. Are you quick on your feet?

RABBIT. Running like?

CAROLINE. Yeah running.

RABBIT. I don't like running.

CAROLINE. Did you hear that Mark?

MARK. I heard it all right. I'm very concerned about it.

RABBIT. Why were you going to enter me in your RUC relay team? Sorry to disappoint but I don't play with the enemy.

CAROLINE. No, this isn't about us. This is about you.

RABBIT. What about me?

CAROLINE. Tell him who called in today.

MARK. About the BMW?

CAROLINE. Rogers? Ring any bells, Rabbit? Rogers? Very well connected. Aren't they?

RABBIT. I don't know nobody called Rogers.

MARK. They're not the UVF Rogers are they?

RABBIT. Fuck off.

CAROLINE. Worse than that.

MARK. It's not the Rogers family that had links with the LVF?

CAROLINE. Is that those really mad bastards'?

MARK. Yeah.

CAROLINE. That's them.

MARK. You don't think that they would be waiting for Rabbit to be released do you?

CAROLINE. I don't know that they would wait that long.

MARK. What do you mean?

CAROLINE. The reason I came in to assist with this investigation, Robert is that I was coming back into the station after lunch time when I noticed a couple of really dodgy looking characters standing outside the main gate. Mumbling, beautiful BMW, blah, blah, like my baby, blah, blah, bloody joyrider blah, blah . . . string them up, blah, blah, blah. Hanging's too good for them.

MARK. And did you think they were the Rogers men?

CAROLINE. I know they were but I didn't know some idiot had stolen their cherished BMW. They loved that car, you know what they're like . . .

RABBIT. They should've invested in a proper security system then.

CAROLINE. People like that have a different view on security, Rabbit. They could probably leave their front doors open and go on holiday for two weeks and when they come back nothing would be touched. The security they have is their reputations. It's like a preventative measure. Nobody is going to be stupid enough to make enemies with these people.

MARK. Is that what you've done Rabbit?

RABBIT. What?

CAROLINE. How long can we keep Rabbit without charging him?

MARK. Not long without applying for an extension.

CAROLINE. What are you going to do then, just let him go?

MARK. Is that what you're recommending?

CAROLINE. I think so.

MARK. If we let him go how would we be sure that he'd be safe?

CAROLINE. That's his problem.

MARK. No, that would be cruel.

RABBIT. Fuck this. I'm not going nowhere until you make those people move away.

MARK. They're free Rabbit. They have every right to be there.

CAROLINE. As does Rabbit if we let him go.

RABBIT. Well I'm not leaving here without an escort.

MARK. Fair enough I'll drop you off at your door.

CAROLINE. Bad idea. What would the neighbours think of that?

RABBIT. Fuck this, go and move those people away first and then I'll make my own way home.

MARK. We can't do that mate. Unless you help us. Then maybe we'll see what we can do about that extension.

RABBIT. Fuck you. Charge me and keep me here.

CAROLINE. Just let him go.

MARK. No. Not after the last time.

RABBIT. What last time?

CAROLINE. Forget about the last time. We've nothing on him. We have to let him go.

RABBIT. I stole a fucking car.

CAROLINE. You've done that millions of times.

RABBIT. And I always get done for it. That's how it works.

CAROLINE. No, you're not dealing with TACT now, you're dealing with us and we never do people for auto crimes, they're too boring. Too many forms to fill in.

RABBIT. I could've killed someone driving like that.

CAROLINE. But you didn't.

MARK. She's right. We have to let you go.

RABBIT. No way. I want police protection. You have to make those people go away before I can go out there.

MARK. I could ask them.

RABBIT. You have to make them.

MARK. They're probably not the Rogers. They're probably not connected. They're probably just two big, big lads out for a bit of a stroll.

CAROLINE. They've been there all night. One of them had something in his hand, maybe something up his sleeve.

RABBIT. A fucking knife.

CAROLINE. No, it wasn't a knife.

MARK. What did it look like?

CAROLINE. More like a screwdriver, maybe. One of those really big ones.

RABBIT. Fuck that.

MARK. He's maybe just going to work.

RABBIT. No way, he's not. He's waiting on me.

MARK. Sure what could he do with a screwdriver?

RABBIT. Plenty.

CAROLINE. Rabbit's right. Remember that guy, what was his name, Ferguson was it? Doesn't matter. You'd know who I mean if you saw the pictures. He was leaning over a fence. Trousers round his ankles. Screwdriver right up . . .

MARK. That was Ferguson.

RABBIT. I've done other stuff.

CAROLINE. He was a mess.

MARK. I saw him. But that was him and he was a bad lad. These guys out here they're probably just going to one of their friends' houses to fix a video or something. Or screw in a few screws. I mean it's not illegal to carry a screwdriver.

CAROLINE. We wouldn't be able to take it off him.

RABBIT. Are you listening to me? I said I've done other stuff.

MARK. For Stanley Brown?

RABBIT. No, just for myself.

MARK. Not interested.

CAROLINE. Come on, you'll have to go.

CAROLINE *moves to the door and opens it.*

MARK. What are you doing?

CAROLINE. I'm going to get him his clothes. He's leaving.

CAROLINE *leaves.*

Corridor

DAVID *stops* BILL *in the corridor with his coat on obviously determined to leave the building.*

DAVID. Where are you going mate?

BILL. I'm going to the pub.

DAVID. Why?

BILL. Take a fucking guess, David son.

DAVID. Bill, if you go out the door you're going to throw away over thirty years of your life.

BILL. I've already done that.

DAVID (*shaking his head*). Come with me.

DAVID *begins to walk towards Interview Room A.*

BILL. Where are we going?

DAVID. We're going to talk to Stanley Brown about that.

BILL. Wait David, I can't go back in there.

DAVID. Yes you can. I'll do all the talking. Trust me mate.

DAVID *opens the door to Interview Room A.*

Interview Room A

STANLEY. Here we go.

DAVID. Good result, Stanley?

STANLEY *watches* DAVID *without really responding.*

DAVID. We get to collar one of the stupid little guys. Robert Montgomery. Society in general will be pleased with that. But you don't care about society in general, you only care about your community, the mighty Protestant community. Maybe your commitment to that community extends only as far as the red, white and blue kerb stones leading out of North Belfast and for all we know those poor, unemployed, uneducated people might even agree with you. I don't. I think we're letting a much more dangerous person go free. They, like you, might think a freedom fighter has won this little battle and is now free to protect them. I want you to know this that when that community turns a blind eye to your criminal activities I will not. When this community blames the British government, Stormont, Sinn Fein or even us for creating people like you. When they see a vacuum where there was once righteousness. When they look at a peace process they see as being a sell-out. When they watch the Nationalist community prosper while they lose jobs, prospects and basic civil liberties. They see the dust settle and they see that void of humanity being filled by men such as you and they hail the future of your organisation as the beginning of the Glory Days of Ulster battling to resist inclusion in an Irish Republic and if that is forced then plotting to bury a hatchet deep in the racist, bigoted heart of the Celtic Tiger. It's all very romantic, the stuff future Hollywood movies may even be made of if anyone outside of North Belfast was foolish enough to see the world through their eyes but they don't and they never will. They see you like I see you. When I look into your eyes I see a reflection of every IRA man you claimed to be protecting us from. I see old men closing their shops and going home penniless because you took their profit and more. I see old ladies cowering in fear trying to forget what they witnessed in case you or your cronies come back to make them forget permanently.

STANLEY. You're looking at the wrong guy. Why not hold that mirror up to yourself and tell me what you see? Tell me what you're doing to protect us.

DAVID. I'm glad you asked. I'm doing my job, playing my part and I'm trying my best to do it the right way.

STANLEY. That's not good enough.

DAVID. You don't think so?

STANLEY. Well I don't feel safe, do you Bill?

DAVID. Not that I'm trying to make you feel less safe but you do know that we have sent the heavy squad in to see Robert Montgomery.

STANLEY. I thought you were the heavy squad.

DAVID. When I left the room he was just about to crack.

STANLEY. And what?

DAVID *watches* STANLEY, *studying his calmness.*

DAVID. You don't give a fuck about Rabbit Montgomery do you . . . because . . . you think it's dead on for joyriding scumbags like him to be in the UDA. I mean I knew the UDA was going down hill but that is just too far.

STANLEY *smiles large.*

STANLEY. You think Rabbit's in the UDA . . . that's what this is all about? (*Laughs.*) Whose fucking genius detective work was that?

DAVID. Rabbit Montgomery is in the UDA.

STANLEY. I mean I knew the RUC was going down hill but that is just . . .

STANLEY *laughs louder.* DAVID *walks away.* BILL *waits, confused.*

Interview Room B

CAROLINE *returns with* RABBIT*'s clothes and places them on the table.*

CAROLINE. Put these on.

MARK. It's too dangerous to let him go Caroline.

RABBIT. I'm going fucking nowhere.

CAROLINE. He can't stay here. Put them on.

RABBIT. I've done bad stuff. Very bad things.

CAROLINE. Who for?

RABBIT. Never mind who for, just take down my statement.

CAROLINE. No.

RABBIT. This is fucking outrageous. I am a dangerous criminal.

CAROLINE. Give me something and I'll make those men go away.

MARK. Who did you steal the car for, Rabbit?

RABBIT. Never mind that.

CAROLINE. Think of it this way. You tell me who made you steal the car and I'll tell the Rogers it must be a vendetta against them and they will forget about you.

MARK. They're like that.

CAROLINE. Who did you steal the car for, Robert?

RABBIT. I can't tell you that.

MARK. Yes you can.

CAROLINE. You have to.

RABBIT. I can't.

CAROLINE. Time is up! Tell me who you stole the car for or get yourself out of my sight.

RABBIT. I told you I can't tell you that.

MARK. So you admit you stole it for someone.

RABBIT. Fuck sake you have to help me here, I just steal cars I don't kill people.

MARK. Who does kill people?

RABBIT. They do.

CAROLINE. Who's they?

RABBIT. I can't tell you that.

    CAROLINE *moves to the door.*

MARK. You better be careful out there.

CAROLINE. Get dressed.

RABBIT. I don't want to go out there.

CAROLINE. Do you want me to help you?

RABBIT. For fuck sake.

CAROLINE. Let's go.

    RABBIT *gets up and gets dressed as* CAROLINE *continues to hurry him up.*

RABBIT. You can't make me leave here. You have to help me.

CAROLINE. You want our help, help us.

MARK. Help yourself.

RABBIT. I want to stay here.

CAROLINE. Who did you steal the car for?

MARK. Tell us and you can stay.

CAROLINE. Come on they're waiting outside.

MARK. Save your life son.

CAROLINE. Come on tell us.

MARK. This is your last chance.

CAROLINE. Who did you steal the car for?

RABBIT. Thompson. Walter Thompson.

CAROLINE *is obviously gutted.* MARK *a little confused.*

MARK. Walter Thompson?

RABBIT. Yeah, he's a UDA guy, he wanted it for another job. I wasn't going to be doing the other job I was just brought in to get the BMW.

CAROLINE *and* MARK *exchange looks of disappointment.*

CAROLINE. Walter Thompson and Stanley Brown?

RABBIT. No just Thompson.

CAROLINE. No, no, no.

MARK. Is that the truth, Rabbit?

RABBIT. And he's asked me to do other stuff too.

MARK. But not Stanley Brown.

RABBIT. No.

MARK. You're not very bright are you Rabbit?

CAROLINE. Have you ever had any dealings with Stanley Brown?

RABBIT. No.

CAROLINE. Has Stanley Brown ever asked you to do anything for the UDA?

RABBIT. No.

CAROLINE. Well if that's true then we're going to have to go after Walter Thompson now and do you know the first thing I'm going to tell him? Robert Montgomery grassed you up. I reckon he's going to be mighty disappointed in you Rabbit.

RABBIT. You can't do that.

CAROLINE. Watch me.

RABBIT. Come on mate, help me out here. You said if I helped you you would help me.

MARK. But you gave us the wrong name.

RABBIT. Don't do this to me.

MARK. Let's go.

CAROLINE. Unless there is something you want to tell us about Stanley Brown.

RABBIT. I don't know nothing about him. He's a mad fucker like but . . .

CAROLINE. You must know something.

MARK. Anything.

CAROLINE. Stanley Brown has threatened hundreds of people where you live, Rabbit? Now do you seriously expect me to believe that you don't know anything about any one of them.

RABBIT. Stanley Brown kills people.

MARK. He's not going to kill you. He's not going to get anywhere near you. You're safe with us.

CAROLINE. Do you know Henry Walker, Walker's Off-licence? Stanley Brown held a gun to his head because he wouldn't hand over his hard earned money so as Stanley could go and drink it with his mates.

RABBIT. Is that supposed to make me feel something? 'Cause I'll tell you all I feel is this. Where will you be when Stanley Brown holds a gun to my head?

MARK. Listen you wee shite. Stanley Brown is holding a gun to all our heads. You give us something on him and we can lock him away for ever.

RABBIT. What world do you live in. I'm saying nothing.

CAROLINE. What about Walter Thompson?

RABBIT. It's like this, I'm more frightened of Stanley Brown than Walter Thompson, the whole Rogers clan or even you.

MARK *grabs* RABBIT *by the back of the neck and forces his face into the table. Holding him there.*

MARK. You're going to tell me everything I need to know in the next five minutes or I'm going to start breaking your limbs.

CAROLINE. What are you doing?

MARK. You heard what he said, he's more frightened of them than us. Step outside for five minutes while I change his mind.

CAROLINE. Step away from him Mark.

MARK. Tell me what you know about Stanley Brown and the UDA. If you don't know anything, make it up but it better be convincing or I'm going to break every bone in your body.

CAROLINE. I said step away now, Mark!

MARK *releases* RABBIT *and steps away, confused.*

RABBIT. I want to see a solicitor immediately. I want to make a complaint against him. I think he's broke my tooth.

CAROLINE. If you want legal representation we can arrange it for you. If you want to make a complaint we can arrange that too.

MARK. Caroline, what are you doing?

CAROLINE. My job.

CAROLINE *pulls up a chair and glares at* RABBIT.

MARK *walks out of Interview Room B and waits in the corridor, fuming, worried and disappointed.*

Interview Room A

DAVID. Did you ever think in your thirty years that it would come to this Bill?

BILL. We're supposed to be on the same side Stanley. I joined the police to fight the IRA and I'm sure you joined the UDA for the same reason.

DAVID. The IRA must be laughing their heads off at us. Loyalist feuds in Portadown. The LVF taking on the UVF and now this. UDA members threatening police officers. Where will it end?

STANLEY. If we're all on the same side what am I doing in here? Why are you not out there catching IRA men?

DAVID. We can't really prosecute them for laughing Stanley.

BILL. If you weren't all gangsters now we wouldn't have to do this.

STANLEY. You can fucking talk. How long have you been on the take?

DAVID. About as long as you've been threatening old ladies.

STANLEY. Fuck you.

DAVID. No fuck you.

STANLEY. What time is it? Start the tape or fuck off.

DAVID. Let's stop the games. I know you've got to Bill, we all do now, so he's useless to you from now on.

BILL. David . . .

DAVID. Shut up Bill. (*To* STANLEY.) I also know you've threatened at least one more of my colleagues and that to me is unacceptable.

STANLEY. I'm shaking.

DAVID. You think you're pretty smart don't you? Name, address, vehicle details, vital statistics. What you seem to forget is that I have all those details on you Stanley and we have the manpower to be all over you every day of your life until you make one little mistake. You could be spending a lot of times in this room for everything from directing terrorism to littering. And let me tell you something else if anything ever happens to my colleague or any member of her family I'll hold you personally responsible. If her daughter falls and cuts her knee I'm going to blame you. If her son falls down the stairs I'm going to blame you.

STANLEY. Yeah, yeah, yeah. Like that'll stand up in court.

DAVID. I'm not talking about court any more Stanley. There's no tape here and these walls are sound proof so I've no problem telling you this. One day you'll have a few drinks in your favourite loyalist club with your scumbag friends, maybe have one too many and come out and start your wee dander home. Maybe you'll be too pissed to hear the car pull up, maybe you won't recognise any of the four men who take you by the scruff of the neck and drag you to the nearest dark alley.

STANLEY. You'll need more than four.

DAVID. One for each arm and one for each leg should be enough for a drunken piece of shit like you. And then . . .

STANLEY. I'm all ears.

DAVID. I'll be there and I will not have a problem making you just another name on a grave stone. Bye, bye Stanley Brown. I'll even stop by your Mum's house and give her the good news.

MARK *enters Interview Room A.*

STANLEY. Hey! I'm glad you're here. I've just been threatened by your fellow officers. Haven't I Bill?

BILL. Saying nothing.

MARK. You're free to go Mr Brown. Get the hell out of my sight.

DAVID. How safe do you feel now?

The End.

A Nick Hern Book

The Force of Change first published in Great Britain in 2000
as a paperback original by Nick Hern Books Limited,
14 Larden Road, London W3 7ST in association with
the Royal Court Theatre, London

The Force of Change copyright © 2000 Gary Mitchell

Gary Mitchell has asserted his right to be identified as the
author of this work

Typeset by Country Setting, Kingsdown, Kent CT14 8ES
Printed and bound in Great Britain by Biddles, Guildford

ISBN 1 85459 616 0

A CIP catalogue record for this book is available from the
British Library